Iona

Images and Reflections

Iona

Images and Reflections

WILD GOOSE PUBLICATIONS
www.ionabooks.com

First published 2007 by

Wild Goose Publications
Fourth Floor, Savoy House, 140 Sauchiehall Street, Glasgow G2 3DH, UK
Wild Goose Publications is the publishing division of The Iona Community
Scottish Charity No. SC003794 Limited Company Reg. No. SC096243

ISBN: 978-1-905010-40-0

A catalogue record for this book is available from the British Library.

Overseas distribution:
Australia: Willow Connection Pty Ltd, Unit 4A, 3-9 Kenneth Road,
Manly Vale, NSW 2093
New Zealand: Pleroma, Higginson Street, Otane 4170, Central Hawkes Bay
Canada: Novalis/Bayard Publishing & Distribution, 10 Lower Spadina Ave., Suite 400,
Toronto, Ontario M5V 2Z2

Produced by Reliance Production Company, Hong Kong
Printed and bound in China

Foreword

While he was praying, his face changed its appearance and his clothes became dazzling white. (Luke 9:29)

I e-mailed David one day from the Wild Goose Publications office to ask him for some shots of Iona (I was looking for images for a new edition of George MacLeod's *The Whole Earth Shall Cry Glory*). Almost immediately, David sent me a folder with over 200 photos. The moment I saw David's photographs I knew they would make a beautiful book. To me, they are not the 'usual' photos of Iona; the predictable ones you see in some tourist books. They have a poetry and a voice. Anja's photographs are the same. Anja deserves her own book. There are fewer photos from her here because she more often works in black and white, or at least did during the period when I was editing this book. If you would like to see more of Anja's photographs visit the Oran Crafts website (www.orancrafts.co.uk) or The Columba Steadings on the isle of Iona.

Because David's and Anja's photographs are so poetic, I naturally thought of the idea of inviting people to compose reflections inspired by them. I sent writers a CD of photos and they chose the images they wanted to write on. All the writers have Iona connections. Most have lived and worked on the island as part of the Iona Community. Thanks to the writers in this book – and to Jane Darroch-Riley of Wild Goose Publications for her skilful, beautiful design work.

If you have been to Iona before, I hope that this book helps you to revisit it. If you have never been, I hope that through it you may visit the island for the first time. More than that, I hope that this book helps you to see differently, and to recognise the poetry of the place you live in here and now. I know that I'll open it on days here at the office when I need to see things differently and to live more in the here and now.

Neil Paynter, Glasgow

Introduction

I was working in the MacLeod Centre on Iona when a group of teenagers arrived. They were greatly unsettled by the fact that they couldn't get a signal for their mobile phones. Thus they were bereft of the affirmation of sending pictures home in the instantaneous way to which they had become accustomed. If you can't picture it, can you be sure you have experienced it? This is the technological alienation of the twenty-first century. I have some sympathy. Since I first came to Iona, it has been an essential part of experiencing a sense of the place that shapes our spirituality to keep on taking pictures; never forgetting that both the one behind the camera and the one who sees the picture become part of the community of seeing.

I used to have to wait, to see how they had turned out. Pop the cartridge out, bend those bizarre retaining tabs on the mailing envelope. Entrust it to the post. With digital, we are spoiled. But who would want to go back? Though the challenge inherent in the volatility of digital media, and the addictive inflation of opportunity to keep on snapping, are accelerating the evolution of our seeing. How will we see next? What will we need to see?

Our Iona pictures unwittingly turn out to be the foundational archives of our lives. Through times of ecstatic joy, of peace, of deep pain and unbelievable frustration. Iona is never a place of escape; rather of catching up with being human. Reviewing these pictures is an emotionally dangerous activity.

This book takes that risk further, as we hand these deeply personal seeings over to others, whose Iona lives have intersected ours. A bit like the old experience of mailing envelopes: you let go in trust. And the writers have delivered: seeing through our lenses, but with their own rich insights sometimes years after the event.

Like scripture, a picture is new every morning. It finds its life in your own seeing; reaches out. May this book touch and enrich your life. And all ours.

David Coleman

Contents

'To be a Christian consists
not in feeling but in following,
not in ecstasy but in obedience.'

William Littleboy, an English Quaker, 1853–1936

This track is a bit like my journey, Jesus –
winding and gravelly,
rather rough at the edges.
But it's well-used too,
cut deep into the earth –
a firm track, going somewhere.
It gives me the confidence I need
to keep going,
always travelling, like you.

'Invisible we see You, Christ beneath us …
In You all things consist and hang together:
The very atom is light energy,
The grass is vibrant,
The rocks pulsate.
All is in flux; turn but a stone and an angel moves …'

George MacLeod, from The Whole Earth Shall Cry Glory

… and so we love the very stones of Your house, Jesus,
literally pulsating with Your life.

… But how may we better love
the bricks and mortar
the steel and cement
the corrugated iron and the cardboard
of Your other houses
in shanty town or city slum …
… or do angels not move there too?

John Harvey

Unaligned,
off-centre,
these arches wonderfully, and with humour,
warn us against
any overweening pride
in the works of our hands.
And pride in the works of our souls? …

From the place where we are right
flowers will never grow
in the spring.

The place where we are right
is hard and trampled
like a yard.
But doubts and loves
dig up the world
like a mole, a plough.
And a whisper will be heard in the place
where the ruined
house once stood.

Yehuda Amichai, Hebrew poet (1924–2000)

What have you caught at Camas, Jesus,
fisher of women and men?
Hard-bitten quarrymen;
    wonderful salmon;
        nervous borstal boys;
            reluctant addicts;
                eager volunteers;
and my heart,
singing in the space
    and the clarity
        and the challenge
of this place of your eternal fishing!
Cast your net here, Jesus,
for as long as the hills and the seas remain!

Originally quarry-workers' cottages, then a salmon-fishing station, the Camas Centre on the Isle of Mull is run by a staff group with specialist skills, helped by several volunteers. Young people from the city and elsewhere, and other groups too, come to Camas for an adventure holiday with outdoor opportunities for canoeing, walking, swimming and camping, a visit to Iona, and the experience of exploring issues, building relationships, and facing new challenges through living and working in community.

John Harvey

Carried over from Ireland
On a dark tide,
Leaving with blood on his hands
Under red skies:
Man, poet, passionate priest
Born of high kings,
Agent of change in the east,

Originator of terrible things:
Find him in armour, find him

In prayer, find him repenting, find him stripped bare:
Only inspired by a battling brief, a
North Country hero who hacked out belief, on
A rock, on an island: the loner:

COLUMBA OF IONA

John Davies

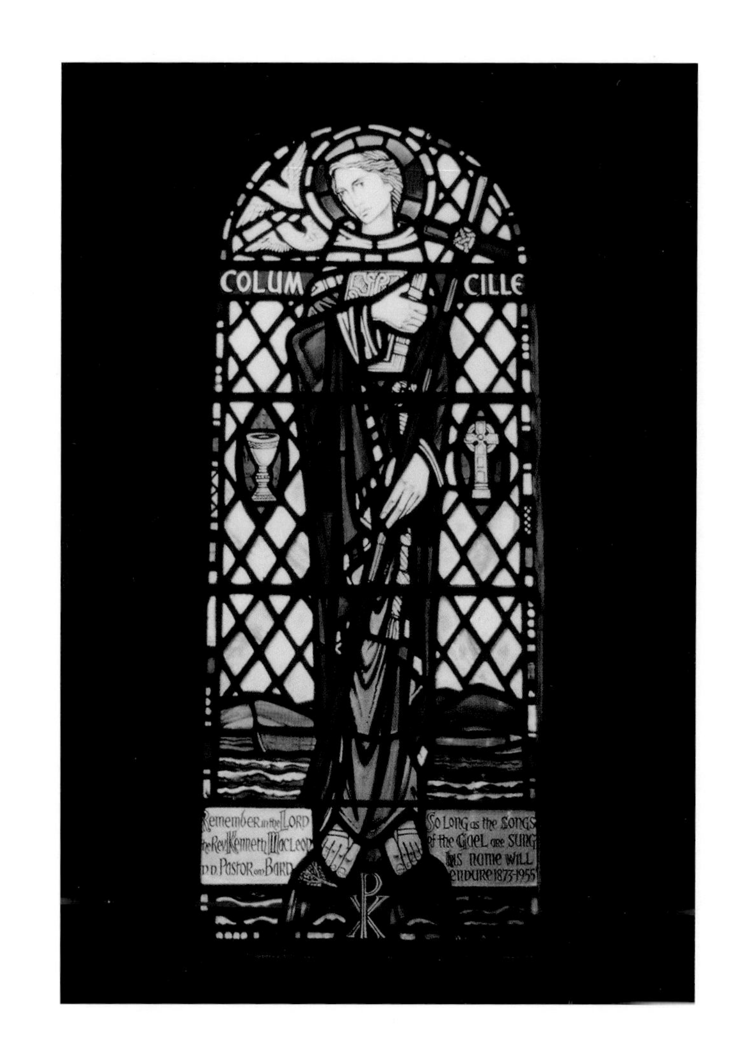
COLUM CILLE
Remember in the LORD
the Rev Kenneth MacLeod
D.D. Pastor and Bard
So long as the songs
of the Gael are sung
his name will
endure 1873-1955

'What you writing in the sand, Daddy?'
I had to ask – cos I can't read yet.
'Thanks,' my daddy said. 'Cos thanks is good.'
Thanks is good, my daddy said …
sand and sea,
my brightest coat and favourite hat,
a daddy who writes with a stick in the sand –
and takes pictures afterwards
of me, happy,
and just wandering
into the middle of my daddy's 'thanks'.

Tom Gordon

How comforting to see the light
that beckons from an open door,
to welcome me with promised truth
that I will find my rest once more
within the bosom of the life
which is community's domain:
my soul embraced within its walls;
my faith and hope and love sustained.

I've lit my candle once again
and, in its flickering glow,
delight to watch the shadows
leap and dance along the wall.
And now, it is no longer mine alone,
but shines for your small corner too,
as light, like love, is shared and spread,
to set your face aglow.

Tom Gordon

The doves fly up when I run by.
I make them fly into the sky.
They're chased away without a cry –
oh, see them rise so high.

The white doves wait till I've run by.
They watch me go with wary eye,
then flutter down from perch on high
in peace – to wonder 'Why?'

It takes patience to wait.
So here I stand, scrubbed and clean,
ready for use, biding my time,
waiting to be filled with good things
that will nurture and nourish people in need.
And then, when they're fed, and I'm empty,
I'll be patient some more,
and wait to be filled up again,
scrubbed and clean, and standing here,
ready for use, biding my time.

Tom Gordon

It seems so long since he has been away,
and yet, it is no time at all.
What will he bring me from his travels
that will be for my delight?
I do not want a successful catch, or treasures from afar.
All I need now is his safe return;
in that, I will rejoice.
For when he has landed once again upon my shore,
I will hold him, and love him, and delight in him
as if it was the very first time.

Atlantic winds will blow
and waves, with threatening might,
will crash upon my shore.
But here I stand on timeless rocks,
that through the ages have withstood
wild nature's force, and yet survive.
So too must I – for certainly,
while on solid ground I stand,
I know that wind and waves
will not overwhelm me now.

Tom Gordon

I

Candlelight
fluttering light,
flittering light;
our little prayers
dancing,
breathing in God's love.

II

Altar candles,
wax and marble,
dancing light on solid stone,
and God,
nearer to us
than breathing.

Ruth Burgess

DO SHEW THE LORD'S DEATH TILL HE

How small is life?
How big is death?
How deep is resurrection?

Always the questions, God,
never the ‘answers’.
Always the changing sky
and the green grass growing.

Ruth Burgess

I

Sometimes the way is steep,
sometimes covered in celandines,
but always the journey.

II

Rucksacks, waterproofs and walking boots.
How does a twenty-first-century pilgrim
let the buttercups tickle her toes?

III

Suitably booted
and well-provisioned
we stride ahead
seeking God's presence:
whilst creation
shouts GLORY!
under our feet.

Ruth Burgess

Often, when living in the Abbey, I would sit quietly in the cloisters early in the morning, as a golden dawn broke over the Sound of Iona. And then a solitary sparrow would share that morning silence and I would ask myself, 'Why does the presence of my feathered friend make this sacred space more special and God's love more real?'

The Scottish sculptor Chris Hall, over several years, created exceptionally beautiful sculptures in stone within the Abbey cloisters. This one powerfully reminds us that as the blood of Christ is shared, somewhere in the world, at every moment of every day, it carries within it both the hope and the continuing agony which permeate our times.

Millions of people believe that Iona is ‘a place of peace’. It is that, and has been through the centuries. Yet it is also a place of ‘uncomfortable peace’ in which God’s energising Spirit constantly propels us to a wider awareness of our broken world: a peace which invites us to walk tenderly on earth, to seek justice and to risk our lives for Christ.

Peter Millar

peace

The local ferry nears the shores of Mull. A few minutes earlier it left Iona perhaps carrying some bikes, luggage, local folk and day visitors. Yet one can say with certainty that some of those people on board have just had a life-changing experience on Iona, and that, as they step ashore on Mull, they know what it means to have felt the healing love of the Creator in a new and amazingly refreshing way.

What is it about these beautiful creatures that calms our souls? Just to watch them, even briefly, is to experience joy in the heart. The mystery and friendship of God is shown in many ways on Iona. In their own delightful way, the Highland cattle illumine our pilgrim journey as they reveal yet another dimension of the glory of creation – a truth understood in the Celtic Church, centuries ago.

Soaring high over the island. Free, yet also disciplined in their flight formation. The wild geese are always powerful signs of that ultimate Spirit which brings life to every human being: the Spirit which enables us to walk in freedom – in the light and truth and possibility of the Gospel each new day.

Peter Millar

Beautiful but short-lived footprints in the sand on one of Iona's glorious white beaches. May they invite us to tread more lightly on the earth, and to do all in our power to save this gloriously diverse planet which, with all creation, is the 'place of our abiding' for a very short time.

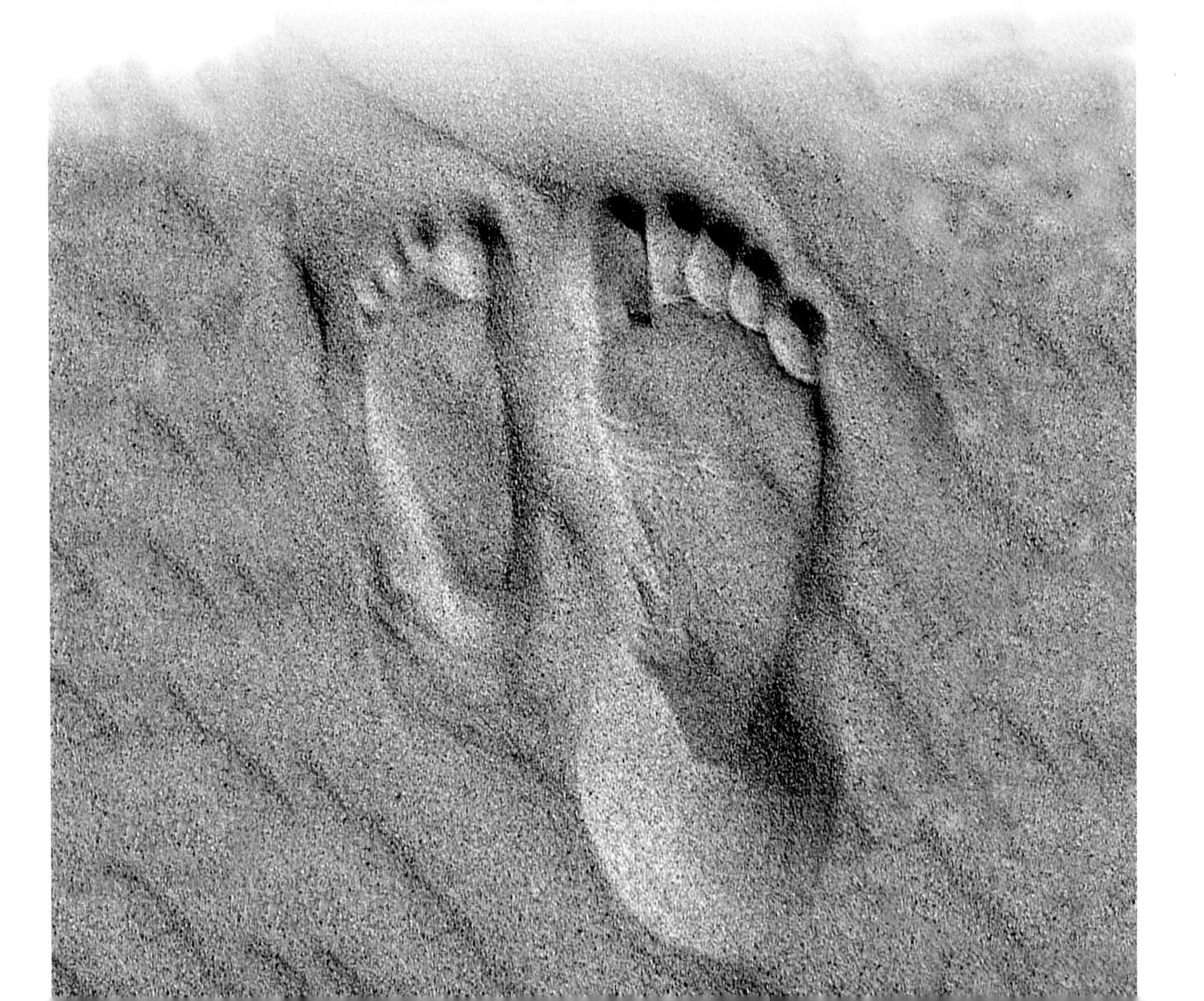

Island of Storm, on a summer's day, with the tide coming in –
standing in exactly the right spot on the sandbar,
weighing exactly the right child-sized amount,
it's possible to be catapulted upwards by the force of the water –
to become part of the rainbow,
to feel the pressure and the power of the waves,
and to collapse in a heap of exhausted giggles,
ready for the next rush.

It's possible.

do I drift
through life
noticing
(as if I should care)
a pattern
emerging,
transient,
in my wake?

or do I
take care to
notice the
constant presence,
patterning,

rock solid,
in the sand?

never the same
for ever the same

heart beating
breathtaking
breathstoppingly
beautiful

pattern
embracing
each day, each
night

Ruth Harvey

Last week I knelt
and received you,
a perfect
flat disc, the surface, neatly
embossed
with what passes,
week by week,
for a cleaned-up cross.

This week someone
good took a knife
and cut you into perfect
cubes of
manufactured bread.

I held out my hands
and square, tidy
and tasteless
it was you I received.

On an island I know
they stir you and scrape you
and knead you, and raise you,
and beat you
and bake you and then
in a boat, with friends,
they break you.

And each of us pulls
at your flesh, pulls
with our bare
begging hands.

For you never come to us
as perfect circle,
or perfect cube.

You are not
a cardboard cut-out
or a mechanical tube,
tamed into
distilling life
on demand.

The gull descending
breaks the air.

With a wing beat

crumble me too.

Alison Swinfen

And so you
love us back
into the earth.

Even when the
lost sheep is
found, spilling
its white
wool over a
raped and bleeding
world, spilling
its guts
into starving
soil, lending its
bones to bleach
in the sunshine
after the
scavenger's kiss.

Even then,
even unto death,

you are the gasp,
the shocked
beat of life,
the stench of the end
which marks
the start

of all things new.

Alison Swinfen

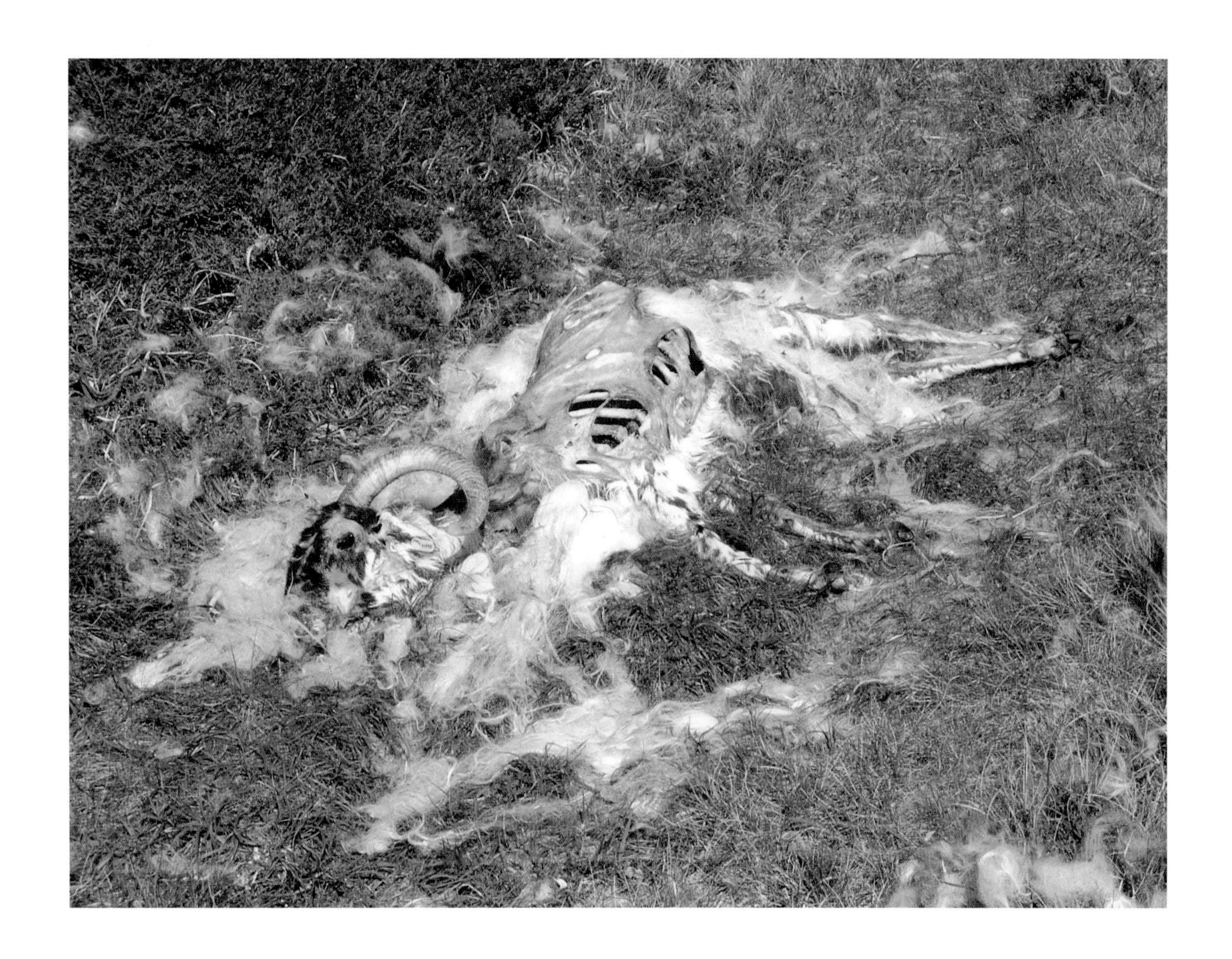

You who are of
candle grease
and tallow,
of the hard
the melting
and the soft.

Of damp wick
of flicker,
you who bring
the occasional
bright splutter.

You who are
the morning after
the light before.

Wait with me when
I trim the wick, and
coax a dampened
fire to flame.

Alison Swinfen

Fan the air fiercely
whenever I
refuse in apathy
to let love burn.

Stick to my fingers,
strike where I'm rough,
spill the liquid of life
of love,

make it messy
make it thick.

Come light,
fire, light.

Come flicker,
come quick.

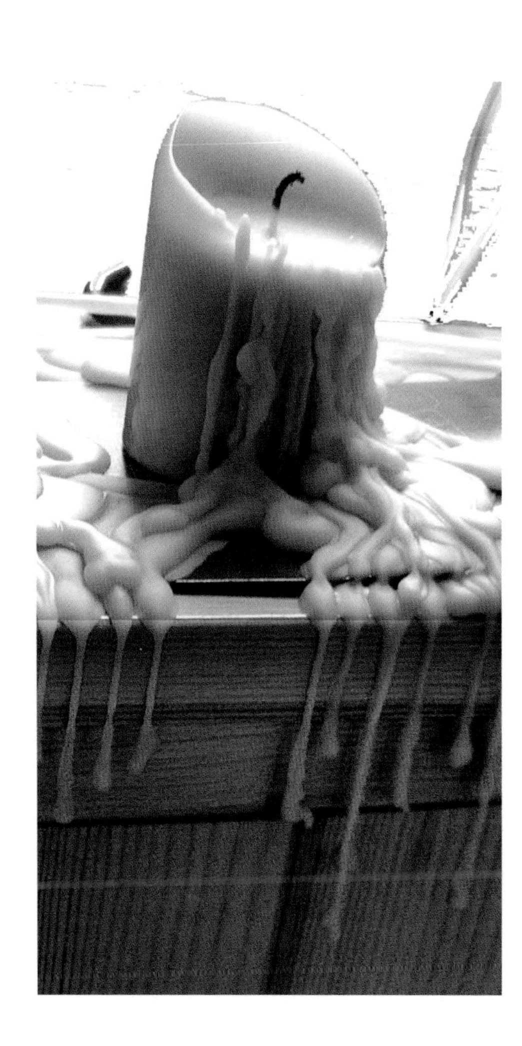

From the beach
we see three
breaking in
like moths
to the light.

Drawn

by the noise
of a heavy catch,
the hard crunch
of a boat
ashore,

by the wood smoke
from the fire,
by the smell of
breakfast and
fresh fish frying.

Alison Swinfen

Once
soft hot rock
cooled
slowly
through decades,
millennia,
while life formed above,
and came
and went
in the light, wind and rain.
Then the sea broke,
ground
and rolled
these pieces
through a few short centuries,
till one day
life lifted
and placed them
here.
Yesterday,
as it were.

David Osborne

Still
in the sun
rain and wind
the stones wait
bound to the earth.
But we can fly.

David Osborne

As it was in the beginning,
rock, water, air and life,
and now us,
watching,
aware,
and waiting.

'On the other side,'
said the man from Nazareth.
'Throw your nets on the other side.'
And curiously
they did
and their lives
changed.

David Osborne

Abraham looked up
and saw three men standing
and he bowed low.

Day off moments: So I run and kick off my shoes to feel the sand and sea between my toes.

Day off moments with no one to call back but oystercatchers and herring gulls.

Nothing to pick up but messages left in the landscape: How sometimes life is like a thousand shades you could never begin to describe. And sometimes life is simply blue sky, green grass, white waves. And it feels like a fight or swing between the two ways of seeing and being sometimes.

Day off moments with no one to get in touch with but my self again.

No deliveries to pick up but what comes to me, what waves leave at my feet: periwinkles, cowrie shells, pieces of coloured glass like precious stones, willow pattern china.

No details to get lost in but the business of a rock pool.
Nothing to follow up but the path of a shore crab.
Nothing to file but ideas for poems.
No services to attend but the wedding of sea and sky.
Nothing to note but the taste and texture and salty, sharp smell of the day.
No one to meet with but the God of silence and solitude.

Day off moments I retreat into to discover new energy. New energy to take back into work.

Neil Paynter

Oyster shells
scallops
periwinkles
whelks
cowrie shells …

Moments turning colours over and contemplating spirals.

Moments like seashells: Like the tiniest, most perfectly wrought seashell you discover on a walk completely lost to yourself, absorbed instead in the miraculous detail of God's world.
Moments you keep wrapped in tissue paper inside a jewellery box.
Carry around and take out to remind yourself. Set on a shelf in your room like upon an altar.

Moments like shells and stones you string around your neck and keep close to your heart.
To show you've lived; been cradled and tossed; stood on the edge dreaming out.
To remind yourself that you are part of God when you feel far away and can't hear or smell the sea.
To show you believe in moments.

Moments like a beautiful stone made up of flecks of mica and sunlight, feldspar, red granite, basalt … fished from a wonderful tide-pool moment.

Moments like a beautiful stone you carry home in your pocket, and take out to see how it's lost its glistering magic on the way, intensity of wet colour – so you try to recapture it.

Neil Paynter

Shine it with spit and taste the salt. Set it in a glass bowl in tap water.

Moments of holding banners of kelp up for the sunlight to shine through –
beautiful as stained glass.

Moments that feel so right: Like a sea-rounded stone in the palm of your hand, perfectly smooth with a good heft.

Moments you carry away with you in your walk. Feeling the good, smooth slide and stretch of bones and joints, feeling comfortable in your skin. Moments your whole body sings. Like a symphony. Like a funk tune.

The spring of machair and the sucking squelch of bog
High cairns
Low, wet patches of cottongrass
Falling asleep between two hills like in the hollow of God's hand
and being woken up by cows.
A path.

No path.

Neil Paynter

The priest who travelled from Mount Athos.
The woman who came from Alaska.

The beautiful old woman I met on the north beach the other day, sitting on a sand dune with a shopping bag, who told me how she'd been trying to get back here for twenty years. 'Heaven, isn't it?' she sighed, watching the waves. And then turned to face the sunset, the red-orange light falling gracefully on her mapped face.

The man I met in the pub one afternoon, who told me he'd been camping alone on Mull and had never felt such peace.

He worked for a big company, he said, and travelled all over the world – Hong Kong, New York, Singapore. 'Know where I was this time last week?' he asked me. 'A strip club in L.A. Know where I was the week before? … Shakespeare in London.' He ordered me a whisky with a nod people noticed, and I went over and joined him.

He sat silent a moment, then began telling me about a woman in his office who had killed herself. She sat a couple desks away; it was busy, but they talked sometimes. No one knew why she did it, they just came in one day and she was gone.

'She was beautiful. Could have had any man she wanted,' he said, and took a drink.

He went camping to get away – bought a tent, one of those camping stoves – to stop, get grounded again. When she killed herself he suddenly became aware of something down inside himself, dying too.

'I just kept seeing her empty desk every place. Know what I mean?' he asked. I nodded.

He gazed out the window; the late afternoon light glowed on the Ross of Mull, on red granite walls and columns; felt like a warm touch – on our hands, on our faces. He closed his eyes and told me that he wanted to come back here and stay longer, he had some questions.

'I went into the Abbey church – I'm not religious or anything. But felt something. I said a prayer. Lit a candle.'

Meanwhile, he'd take it around with him, he said – the peace he found, the moment he spent. 'Like a still centre. Glowing down inside yourself. Know what I mean?' he asked. I nodded.

We spoke a little longer; he was dying to tell someone he said. He ordered me another malt whisky; got up and went out on the small talk left. I could see him out the window. Standing, staring out at the sea.

I thought about all he'd told me, and about how much of my time I spend flying around, or sitting closed-up in a corner. Like God was telling me that if I just stopped, just glanced up from me a moment, there was a world of deep experience and communion waiting. People behind newspapers and office desks dying to talk, sunsets ripe as fruit. Life in all its fullness.

I became aware of the choice of every moment: Looking up, or looking down. Reaching out, or folding in. Flying away, or standing firm. Feeling, or unfeeling.

Living or dying.

Neil Paynter

Moments when the landscape says you are too hard-hearted.
Moments when you finally come to see the sea after all the rocks and hills you've climbed.

Moments when the sky says open up, says if you can't appreciate the beauty and magic and mystery here on this sacred isle what chance do you have back in the 'everyday' world? When the sky says: Stop and look at me stop and look you are going to die.

The rainbow: pledge of God's promise to be with us.
Through the rain,
in the pain;
reassuring us that love and warmth and light return,
for always there is hope.

The rainbow: icon of God's broad love.
Welcoming all creation
in a celebration of joy.
Each colour alone is beautiful and bright
but together – what a statement. WOW!

God of rainbows,
confront the cynical.
Blow away the blasé.
Fill us with delight,
that we may celebrate the WOW!
In every person, every place.

Zam Walker

The weathered female figures sit,
unnoticed and unnamed.
Claimed and praised by pagans
– yet crouching only on churches.

Female power using sexuality to keep evil at bay.
Or guarding the portals to protect the sacred?

Remind us that the Spirit is at work through our bodies,
that our sexuality is holy,
that nothing reflecting God can be profane.

Zam Walker

Help me to be really present where I am:
unhurried and absorbed,
examining the beauty of each grain of sand;
appreciating the unique texture, colour and smell;
marvelling at the intricacy in apparent simplicity;
living fully now – this second –
ever mindful of the wonder of the moment.

Zam Walker

What joy to paddle in bracing water,
feeling the splash of waves,
squidging sand with our toes,
knowing that we are held in love.

What faith to take a chance,
plunging into new experiences,
venturing into the unknown,
trusting that we are held in love.

Dare us always to be open to the new,
braving the unexpected,
facing our fears,
discovering with delight that we are held in love.

Zam Walker

As we gathered
to witness for peace
I was reminded
of that other feast on the beach:
Jesus transforming the everyday
with a barbecue breakfast.

Christ, come ashore;
meet us where we are.
Set us up for the days ahead.
And transform us
that the world may be transformed.

Zam Walker

In July 2005, G8 leaders met behind police barricades and barbed wire in Gleneagles, Scotland. During their summit there were nationwide Make Poverty History marches, protests and concerts in which millions of ordinary people took part, calling for the dropping of Third World debt and unfair trade rules that favour the rich – for a more just and peaceful world. On Iona, on the day of the marches, the Iona Community encouraged guests, day visitors and staff to make clay figures of themselves – and to join in a symbolic march around the cloisters of the Abbey.

The figures march around the place of the common life,
demonstrating that all creation cries out against injustice.
The figures, standing proxy for their creators,
invite passers-by to add to their number,
challenging those who see poverty as
something that intrudes on their spiritual quest,
something that untidies their place of pilgrimage,
something apart from peace.

'People come to Iona looking for peace and quiet, and go away seeking peace and justice.'

A volunteer with the Iona Community

Zam Walker

With each rooted
twist and turn,
life is claimed,
greening celebrated:
tenacious journey
of faithful ivy.

Send my roots, Lady,
soft but sure –
succoured life
in your mystery:
tentative journey
of frightened child.

Chris Polhill

Will even gentle tides
wash away peace again?
Peace yearned for,
lost to waves of
subtle change.

Peace worked for,
lost to shifting
perceptions; silence;
doing nothing while others move.

Write peace on our hearts, Lord Jesus,
peace flowing through blood and soul.
So shifting sand
or gentle waves
will never
erase the struggle for your peace.

Chris Polhill

Peace

Sunlight glints on water,
light lines revealing depth –
ever-changing pattern.

Constant living movement
yet eternal sea
holding reflective gaze.

Drawing deeper within,
life's patterns dancing,
God's glancing illumes.

Chris Polhill

Land or sea, the edge uncertain,
between-worlds-place
like dusk and dawn:
you draw me towards,
inwards, along,
with your hidden rock seats,
sometimes at sea's edge,
sometimes sand.
North shore dreaming.

Walk the earth sea sometime place,
listen to its music
from creation's morn:
you sound charm me,
musing, drowsing,
with waves sand-swished,
rock-swirled and hushing,
no rushing.
North shore greeting.

Chris Polhill

Hear the Spirit whisper within,
silent words of loving;
sorrow's tears shared:
you deep touch me,
gently, slowly,
with veil-lift-mystery,
heaven's earth shoreline,
glimpse fleeting.
North shore healing.

Here, in a place of peace,
a strange image:
a human hand resting on the hilt of a sword.
In this sanctuary, ideally,
weapons were banned;
where men from the turbulent world
entered empty-handed, humble,
there could be no armed response.

Yet when the great dead, way back,
were laid in state, even here
it was with their weapons:
signifying status and power over others,
even in the impotence of death.
Archaic priorities, strange bedfellows
with the words 'rest in peace'.

Pride and fear, profit and power,
shaping human lives. Then and now.
'An ideal world would be one
without nuclear weapons.
But we don't live in an ideal world,'
I heard the politician say, today.

And perilously, it doesn't take much
to put any of us on our guard.
Whatever presses our buttons,
we're quick on the draw:
hand jumping to the sword-hilt,
trigger, detonator, send key.

Even when weapons
(whether for defence or attack)
like this great two-handed sword
become obsolete, there are still words –
equally sharp-edged – to wound and destroy.

So, restless, in a far from ideal world,
we're still looking for peace with justice.

Dear God, help us
to lay down our arms
but not to rest – yet.

Jan Sutch Pickard

High windows
at the west end:
in high summer
thin glass is no
impediment, and
the stone heart
of the nave warms
to evening light
pouring through
richly, generously –
like a blessing.

Deep in winter
in dark days
and long nights,
it's bone-cold,
candles burn low;
while hailstones
batter the Abbey,
gales shake glass
but cannot break
this fragile shield –
like a blessing.

Height, depth,
only a narrow
divide between
sanctuary, chaos;
sheltering wings,
when time's right,
will open in flight;
in-between space
letting in the light;
such a thin place –
paradox, blessing.

Jan Sutch Pickard

In this safe and sheltering place
we pause, God, aware of your presence
in the darkness and stillness,
and in the radiance of morning light
which is reflected in the long table,
and held in the steady candle flame.

We can smell the smoke
of other candles, just put out
when the service ended;
we can feel the warmth
of human beings, who have gone out
to the worship of a day's work.

We give thanks
for this handful of folk
who keep faith – all winter long –
through the daily office,
in light, in darkness,
praying for healing,
breaking bread.

And we share
in their prayers for that wider world –
dazzling, dangerous and distracting –
a world in which you are also present
and to which they and we must return:
going out from this sheltering place,
with its gentle darkness,
steadfast stillness.

Amen

Jan Sutch Pickard

Photo Credits and Acknowledgements

Photos on pages 6, 19, 29, 31, 84, 85, 117 by Anja Grosse-Uhlmann
Anja Grosse-Uhlmann is a photographer, cook and mother living on Iona.

All other photos by David Coleman.
David Coleman is a URC minister, a member of the Iona Community, a digital artist and a writer.

'The Place Where We Are Right' from *The Selected Poetry of Yehuda Amichai,* trans. Chana Bloch and Stephen Mitchell (Berkeley: University of California Press, 1996). Used by permission of University of California Press and Chana Bloch.

Ruth Burgess is an Iona Community member who lives in Sunderland with a black-and-white cat.

John Davies is a member of the Iona Community, born and still living on the Irish Sea coast, in Liverpool.

Tom Gordon has been a member of the Iona Community since 1973, is a writer and trainer, and works as hospice chaplain with Marie Curie Cancer Care in their Edinburgh hospice.

John Harvey is a member of the Iona Community, and was once the Warden of the Abbey and the cook at Camas (not at the same time!). He now lives in Glasgow, in active retirement.

Ruth Harvey is the editor of *Coracle,* the magazine of the Iona Community. She lives in Cumbria.

Peter Millar is a writer and campaigner on global issues. He is a former Warden of Iona Abbey and lived and worked in India for many years.

David Osborne is a member of the Iona Community and an Anglican minister living and working near Glastonbury in Somerset.

Neil Paynter lived and worked on Iona for four years as part of the Iona Community's Resident group. He worked in homeless shelters and as a nurse's aide before that. Now he edits books.

Chris Polhill runs the Reflection Gardens in Staffordshire, and is a priest in the Church of England.

Jan Sutch Pickard is a writer, storyteller and former Warden of Iona Abbey.

Alison Swinfen is a member of the Iona Community and is also a Professor of Languages and Intercultural Studies at the University of Glasgow.

Zam Walker is a URC minister in Brighton and a member of the Iona Community; she is partner to David and mother of Taliesin (8) and Melangell (5). She continues to hope that the Church will celebrate God's wonderful diversity in creation through becoming truly inclusive. Her particular passion is exploring issues of body theology through workshops, liturgies and writing.

The Iona Community is:

- An ecumenical movement of men and women from different walks of life and different traditions in the Christian church
- Committed to the gospel of Jesus Christ, and to following where that leads, even into the unknown
- Engaged together, and with people of goodwill across the world, in acting, reflecting and praying for justice, peace and the integrity of creation
- Convinced that the inclusive community we seek must be embodied in the community we practise

Together with our staff, we are responsible for:

- Our islands residential centres of Iona Abbey, the MacLeod Centre on Iona, and Camas Adventure Centre on the Ross of Mull;

and in Glasgow:

- The administration of the Community
- Our work with young people
- Our publishing house, Wild Goose Publications
- Our association in the revitalising of worship with the Wild Goose Resource Group

The Iona Community was founded in Glasgow in 1938 by George MacLeod, minister, visionary and prophetic witness for peace, in the context of the poverty and despair of the Depression. Its original task of rebuilding the monastic ruins of Iona Abbey became a sign of hopeful rebuilding of community in Scotland and beyond. Today, we are about 250 Members, mostly in Britain, and 1500 Associate Members, with 1400 Friends worldwide. Together and apart, 'we follow the light we have, and pray for more light'.

For information on the Iona Community contact:
The Iona Community, Fourth Floor, Savoy House, 140 Sauchiehall Street,
Glasgow G2 3DH, UK. Phone: 0141 332 6343
e-mail: ionacomm@gla.iona.org.uk; web: www.iona.org.uk

For enquiries about visiting Iona, please contact:
Iona Abbey, Isle of Iona, Argyll PA76 6SN, UK. Phone: 01681 700404
e-mail: ionacomm@iona.org.uk

Wild Goose Publications, the publishing house of the Iona Community established in the Celtic Christian tradition of Saint Columba, produces books, tapes and CDs on:

- holistic spirituality
- social justice
- political and peace issues
- healing
- innovative approaches to worship
- song in worship, including the work of the Wild Goose Resource Group
- material for meditation and reflection

If you would like to find out more about our books, tapes and CDs, please contact us at:

Wild Goose Publications
Fourth Floor, Savoy House
140 Sauchiehall Street,
Glasgow G2 3DH, UK

Tel. +44 (0)141 332 6292
Fax +44 (0)141 332 1090
e-mail: admin@ionabooks.com

or visit our website at
www.ionabooks.com
for details of all our products and online sales

CW00431496

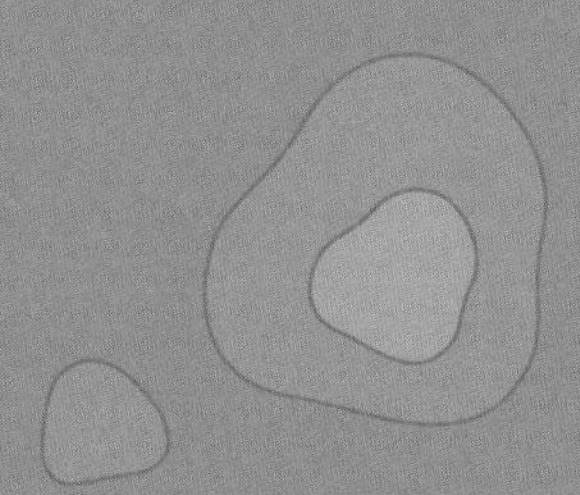

Atlas
DES PRÉJUGÉS

Direction éditoriale : Jean-Baptiste Bourrat
Coordination éditoriale : Maude Sapin
Mise en page : Sandra Fauché
Révision : Emmanuel Dazin
Photogravure : Taïga Media, Paris

Pour la version originale :
Texte, illustrations et design : Yanko Tsvetkov
Polices : *Open Sans* (Steve Matteson), *PT Sans* (ParaType), *Caesar Dressing* (Owen Window), *Julee* (Julian Tunni), *Uncial Antiqua* (Astigmatic)

ISBN : 978-2-35204-359-1
Dépôt légal : septembre 2014

Édition originale en anglais publiée aux États-Unis par Alphadesigner.

Éditions des Arènes
27 rue Jacob
75006 Paris
Tél. : 01 42 17 47 80
arenes@arenes.fr

Atlas des préjugés se prolonge sur les sites
www.arenes.fr
www.alphadesigner.com
www.atlasofprejudice.com

YANKO TSVETKOV

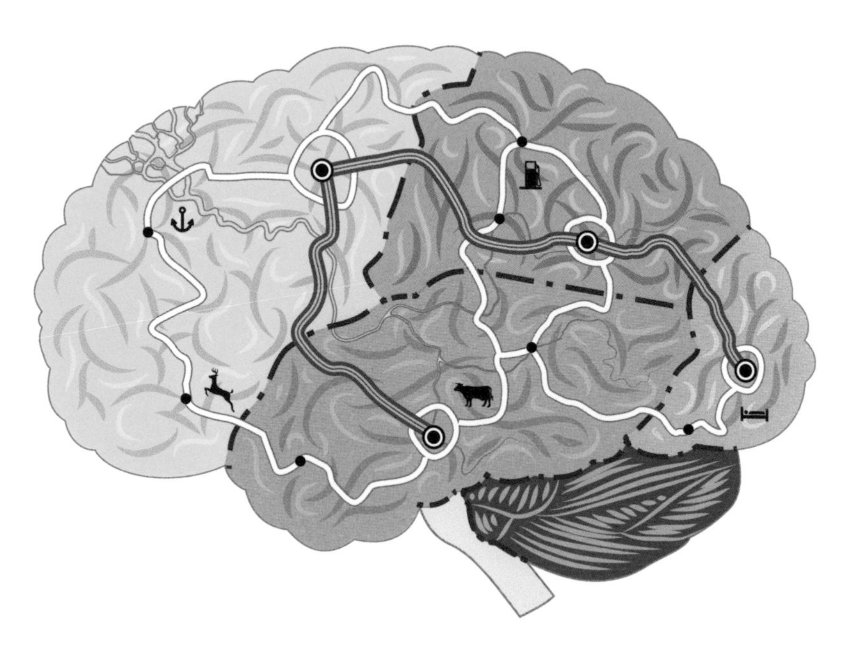

Atlas
DES PRÉJUGÉS

Traduction Jean-Loup Chiflet
avec Christiane Courbey

les arènes

« Aristote affirmait que les femmes ont moins de dents que les hommes ;
il s'est marié deux fois et pourtant il ne lui est jamais venu à l'idée
d'examiner les bouches de ses épouses pour vérifier. »

Bertrand Russell

SOMMAIRE

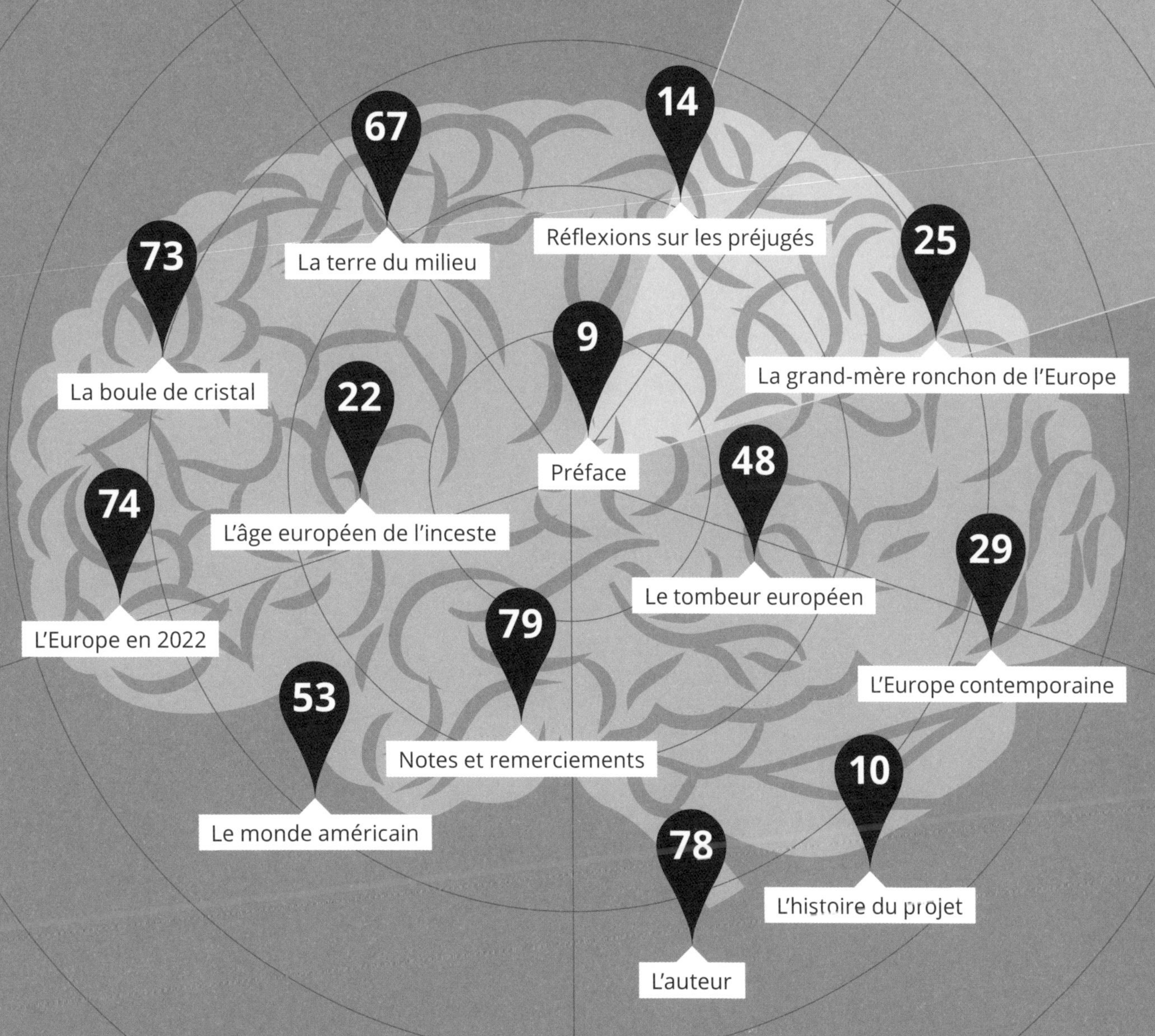

PRÉFACE

Et puis un jour il fait moins chaud. On est fin août. Je ne parle pas du mois d'août allemand mais du mois d'août espagnol. Celui qui vous frit la peau si vous l'exposez au soleil pendant plus d'une minute. Qui vous assomme avec les vents du Sahara, ces vents brûlants qui vous font dégouliner de sueur. C'est la fin des vacances en Europe, enfin... pour ceux qui ont la chance d'avoir un job et qui ont besoin de l'oublier une fois par an.

Mon compte Twitter explose, saturé par les jérémiades de mes amis anglais et allemands : c'est un temps exécrable qui les accueille à leur retour. J'ai envie de leur répondre qu'ils n'ont pas le droit de regretter la chaleur. Parce que transpirer comme un fou pendant une semaine, ça a peut-être du bon, mais quand ça dure tout un été, c'est franchement horrible.

Mon agent littéraire devra attendre jusqu'à lundi pour la première version de ce livre. Il y a des passages tellement disparates... Certains sont trop personnels, d'autres ne sont qu'un charabia *freestyle* produit dans le désordre de mon cerveau en ébullition.

Je ne peux m'en prendre qu'à moi-même. C'est moi qui ai voulu tout rédiger au lieu de demander de l'aide. J'ai une certaine expérience de l'écriture mais c'est mon premier livre. Alors ne m'assommez pas si vous le trouvez nul, je pleure facilement.

D'après un de mes amis, ce besoin de tout faire par moi-même trahit mon narcissisme. Tous mes amis sont francs et honnêtes, et leur avis m'est précieux. Mais celui-là se trompe. Il n'a rien compris. Il ne sait pas que ce que je cherche : en plus de la gloire et de la fortune que ce livre m'apportera, c'est l'occasion de poursuivre la conversation commencée début 2009, quand j'ai réalisé la première carte de mon *Mapping Stereotypes Project*.

Yanko Tsvetkov
Valence, août 2012

L'HISTOIRE DU PROJET

On était en janvier. Un janvier bulgare et non pas espagnol. Tout était couvert de neige, le linge que ma mère avait étendu à son balcon était complètement gelé. Une petite culotte, maltraitée par le vent violent, battait contre la fenêtre avec la régularité alarmante d'un métronome. Toc, toc, toc... Le feu crépitait dans la cheminée. Mon amie Birgit venait de m'écrire de Berlin : juste quelques lignes pour me demander si je n'avais pas froid et si je n'étais pas à la rue. Son « Réponds-moi vite ! » trahissait son inquiétude. Quelques minutes après, un autre copain m'envoyait à peu près le même message. D'Espagne, cette fois.

Me croyant victime d'une catastrophe naturelle, ils se demandaient si je n'étais pas mort... En fait ce qui arrivait était on ne peut plus banal. Cette catastrophe n'était rien d'autre qu'une histoire de politique étrangère. Comme le président Poutine n'était pas content du gouvernement ukrainien pro-occidental, il avait eu recours à l'arme de persuasion massive : le gaz naturel. En stoppant l'approvisionnement des pipelines qui traversent l'Ukraine il faisait pression non seulement sur l'Ukraine mais sur toute l'Union européenne à laquelle appartenaient la plupart des pays concernés. Génial !

Mes amis étaient informés de la crise par les médias mais beaucoup avaient du mal à en comprendre la raison. C'est normal, car l'analyse politique est rarement passionnante. C'est en pensant à eux que j'ai eu idée d'une carte satirique. Je l'ai croquée en un rien de temps. Je l'ai publiée sur un site de partage de photos et les internautes m'ont vite envoyé leurs commentaires. Mais comme je faisais des cartes depuis mon plus jeune âge je n'ai pas accordé trop d'importance à leurs réactions. Pour moi cette carte n'était qu'une blague qu'on dessine et qu'on oublie.

Un an et demi plus tard, j'attendais une voiture devant mon domicile londonien. Emiliano, mon ami vénézuélien, était là pour me soutenir dans ce moment difficile. Si vous aviez vu mon visage vous auriez pensé que je me rendais à un enterrement. Si vous aviez vu le visage d'Emiliano, vous auriez pensé qu'on avait gagné au Loto.

En fait, j'allais être interviewé à la BBC au sujet de cette fameuse carte. Et si nos expressions étaient si différentes, ce n'était pas seulement parce que j'allais passer à la télé : comme tout Slave qui se respecte, mon imagination dérape facilement et je me voyais déjà en train d'avaler ma langue et me couvrir de ridicule. Quant à lui et son psyché latino-américain, il était émoustillé à la perspective d'un moment exceptionnel dédié à mon projet.

Dans ma tête, il fallait absolument que j'évite ce trajet en voiture avec chauffeur. Car en plus d'être slave j'avais grandi

L'EUROPE EN 2009 (MA PREMIÈRE CARTE)

BJÖRK

Notre autre mer à tous

PÊCHEURS ÉGOÏSTES

Cimetière de sous-marins

Golfe d'ABBA

EMPIRE PARANO DU PÉTROLE

Mer banale

EPO

CÉSIUM 137

UNION DES AGRICULTEURS SUBVENTIONNÉS

VOLEURS DE GAZ NATUREL

Mer pas banale

ROUMANIE DU NORD

BANQUE

CANDIDAT À L'UE

CLIVAGES ÉTHNIQUES

LA CHANTEUSE LEPA BRENA

Mer sans or noir

VITICULTEURS ARMÉS

SANS NOM

PAYS SANS YOUTUBE

ÉTAT VOYOU

Notre mer à tous

CHAOS

ACCROS À LA GUERRE

USA

dans l'idéologie communiste qui encourage l'autonomie de l'individu. D'où mon malaise ce jour-là : en acceptant de me faire véhiculer dans Londres au lieu de me débrouiller seul, je jouais le jeu du capitalisme.

Quand elle m'a proposé de m'envoyer une voiture pour me rendre à la BBC, l'assistante a eu du mal à comprendre ma réticence : j'ai marmonné que j'adorais marcher, que prendre le métro était un vrai bonheur, et que je n'avais rien contre le bus... Elle pleurait presque quand elle m'a demandé, désespérée : « Mais enfin pourquoi vous ne voulez pas d'une voiture ? »

Elle ne comprenait pas mon refus, mais comme je ne voulais pas qu'elle me prenne pour un individu malpoli, j'ai capitulé et je lui ai donné mon adresse.

Le chauffeur est venu nous chercher dans une grosse Peugeot noire. Je n'ai jamais rencontré de Kenyan plus aimable que lui. Pour être franc, c'est même le seul Kenyan que j'aie jamais vu. Il nous a demandé sur quoi on allait être interviewés.

Emiliano répondit à ma place : « On va parler de cartes sur les préjugés nationaux », car il savait que j'étais incapable de parler.

« Hmmm ! Ça m'intéresse ! Je peux les voir ? »

Même si je n'avais jamais fait de carte satirique sur le Kenya j'étais extrêmement mal à l'aise. Ma nervosité était telle que j'imaginais mon chauffeur en train de jeter mon cadavre dans la Tamise. Et comme je ne voyais pas Emiliano dans mon délire, j'avais des doutes : avait-il pris part au meurtre ? ou s'était-il enfui par la fenêtre juste avant que je cesse de respirer ? Il est vrai que la paranoïa rend poétique, parfois.

Pourtant, ce n'était pas uniquement le produit de mon imagination. Car quelques minutes avant de partir j'avais téléphoné à ma mère en Bulgarie pour l'informer de la bonne nouvelle. Voilà quelle avait été sa réaction : « Fais attention à ce que tu vas dire ! Tu ne vas pas nous faire honte, hein ? » Ma mère avait grandi – et vécu – sous le communisme. À l'époque il était aussi dangereux de faire des blagues politiques que de fumer de la marijuana. On risquait la prison, tout simplement.

C'est ce qui était arrivé à un oncle de mon père. Plus tard, il a essayé de s'échapper de derrière le Rideau de fer : pour cela il a traversé une rivière à la frontière yougoslave en emmenant sa femme et sa fille de quatre ans avec lui. Résultat : tous les membres de la famille de mon père ont été considérés par le régime communiste comme des traîtres potentiels. Ils ont donc appris à se taire. D'où le mutisme sur l'histoire de cet oncle : j'avais huit ans quand on me l'a racontée. Ma grand-mère m'a dit un jour qu'on avait de la famille en Allemagne. D'après elle, c'était bien que je le sache, mais il valait mieux que je n'en parle pas trop.

Puis ma grand-mère m'a montré une petite boîte rouge dans laquelle elle avait gardé toutes les cartes que l'oncle de mon père avait envoyées. Il y en avait d'Allemagne, du Liban, d'Afrique, d'Hawaï, d'Arizona, de Californie, du Kenya... Que des endroits inconnus pour moi. Ou presque. Je me souviens avoir demandé à ma tante si je pouvais aller en Italie.

« Non ! C'est un pays capitaliste ! »

À l'époque, il était interdit d'aller dans des pays capitalistes. À mon avis c'était dommage parce que « Italie » était un mot si beau. Ma tante m'a aussi expliqué que sur une carte le pays ressemble à une immense botte. D'après elle, à un moment donné il a failli devenir communiste mais, heureusement, il est resté dans la sphère d'influence américaine. Ça m'a rendu triste. J'ai même eu l'idée de libérer l'Italie, un jour.

Comme je n'avais pas beaucoup de livres illustrés, je me contentais des atlas que mes grands-parents gardaient précieusement à la cave. Chaque fois que ma grand-mère descendait chercher un pot de confiture, je la suivais. Comme j'avais peur du noir, c'était le seul moyen d'approcher ces boîtes remplies de livres sans risquer d'être dévoré par le monstre effrayant qui se terrait derrière le mur de briques. Je n'avais droit qu'à un ou deux livres à la fois.

Elle ne tenait sans doute pas à les trouver éparpillés partout dans la maison. D'où ces voyages fréquents à la cave pour y chercher de la confiture.

Je prenais un atlas, le posais ouvert contre la fenêtre, recouvrais la page d'une feuille blanche. Comme je voyais à travers il m'était facile de reproduire les contours. Mais je me suis vite rendu compte que les frontières se déplaçaient avec le temps.

Il y avait des atlas historiques qui décrivaient les différents empires coloniaux. Quelle surprise d'apprendre que l'Afrique était sous le contrôle des nations européennes ! Pour l'enfant que j'étais, ça ne tenait pas debout.

Plus tard, j'ai mieux compris le concept . Mais de savoir que la Bulgarie n'avait pas de colonies me rendait triste. Qu'à cela ne tienne, il me suffisait d'inventer des cartes pour remédier à la situation. J'avais un faible pour Nauru, ne comprenant pas en quoi une petite île perdue dans le Pacifique aurait pu intéresser qui que ce soit. Je l'ai donc répartie entre plusieurs pays qui, dans mon esprit d'enfant, seraient les alliés de la Bulgarie. Parmi eux il y avait l'Italie. Je pris soin d'écrire son nom correctement. Le résultat était génial.

La Bulgarie n'a peut-être jamais eu d'empire colonial mais je savais que sa superficie avait rétréci au cours des siècles. Mon professeur d'Histoire nous avait dit qu'au Xe siècle le royaume bulgare était le plus puissant de la péninsule des Balkans.

Tous les matins, à l'école, on nous faisait chanter un chant qui commémorait le siège de Constantinople par le tsar de Bulgarie. En principe les régimes communistes évitaient de louer les monarchies mais là, ça ne posait aucun problème. Comme notre souverain Kroum n'avait finalement pas pu monter à l'assaut, le chant ne se terminait évidemment pas sur une note victorieuse. Il n'empêche qu'il nous remontait le moral et qu'il renforçait notre sentiment d'identité. À ce sujet, nos profs d'Histoire avaient le souci de faire naître en nous ce sentiment, et de le renforcer. Car nous ne devions pas nous contenter d'examiner des faits, il fallait que nous nous sentions engagés émotionnellement. Chaque fois qu'un empereur byzantin tuait des soldats bulgares, nous nous devions d'être choqués et furieux contre lui. Et chaque fois que notre roi exterminait des troupes byzantines, nous étions fiers et heureux.

En 2009, quand j'ai commencé à étoffer mon projet de cartographie des stéréotypes, beaucoup de gens croyaient que j'avais un fichier politique secret qui me permettait de régler mes comptes. Bizarrement, leur sens de l'identité nationale était très fort. Bien que dispersés dans le monde, ils étaient unis par leur foi en leur pays. Et ils ne toléraient pas que celui-ci fasse l'objet de plaisanteries.

RÉFLEXIONS SUR LES PRÉJUGÉS

Avant que le poète italien Girolamo Fracastoro n'invente le mot *syphilis* à l'époque de la Renaissance, on ne savait pas comment appeler cette maladie honteuse. Chaque peuple se renvoyait la balle en réinventant son origine : c'était une *maladie française* pour les Italiens, les Allemands et les Polonais, *italienne* pour les Français, *espagnole* pour les Hollandais, *polonaise* pour les Russes, et tout simplement *chrétienne* pour les Turcs ottomans.

En fait, la bactérie *Treponema pallidum* sévissait au hasard car elle était bien incapable de reconnaître l'appartenance ethnique de l'organisme qu'elle attaquait. Et ses appellations diverses étaient probablement inspirées par les rivalités politiques qui sévissaient à l'époque. La France était le plus grand ennemi du Saint-Empire romain, immense mosaïque de petites principautés d'Allemagne et d'Italie. Au nord, les Pays-Bas étaient en rébellion contre l'Espagne, et la Pologne contre la Russie. Quant à l'Empire ottoman, il ne voyait dans le reste du continent qu'un ramassis d'États gouvernés par des infidèles à la moralité douteuse. Car la propagande politique n'est pas une invention moderne et les rivalités ethniques ont toujours été propices à une explosion débridée de stéréotypes.

La notion d'étranger comme incarnation du mal a toujours été le centre de gravité autour duquel l'identité tribale s'est élaborée. Elle s'est peu à peu ancrée dans les traditions et les rituels religieux de chaque société. L'objectif des premières guerres était bien défini : il s'agissait de capturer et de tuer le chaman ennemi, cet initié qui avait été choisi par ses frères superstitieux pour être l'intercesseur entre eux et les forces mystérieuses de l'Univers.

Ceux qui proclament que la prostitution est le plus vieux métier du monde ignorent que le chamanisme lui est antérieur : le chaman n'était pas seulement un charlatan *freelance* qui abusait des naïfs. Un portrait aussi réducteur serait une insulte à la responsabilité herculéenne que ces individus portaient sur les épaules.

On attendait des chamans qu'ils aident à comprendre le monde et à lui donner un sens. Ils étaient censés expliquer pourquoi le Soleil réapparait chaque jour, pourquoi l'eau tombe du ciel, pourquoi vos fesses vous démangent si vous ne vous essuyez pas correctement, pourquoi les abeilles adorent butiner les fleurs, et j'en passe, les questions étant plus embarrassantes les unes que les autres. Le chaman avait la clé du savoir, lui seul pouvait expliquer l'inexplicable. Mais il n'en était pas moins homme, et ce ne sont pas les bonbons mais les joints qui lui apportaient le réconfort. Pas étonnant, alors, si son portrait stéréotypé le représente en train de fumer.

LE MONDE VU PAR LE PREMIER ÊTRE HUMAIN

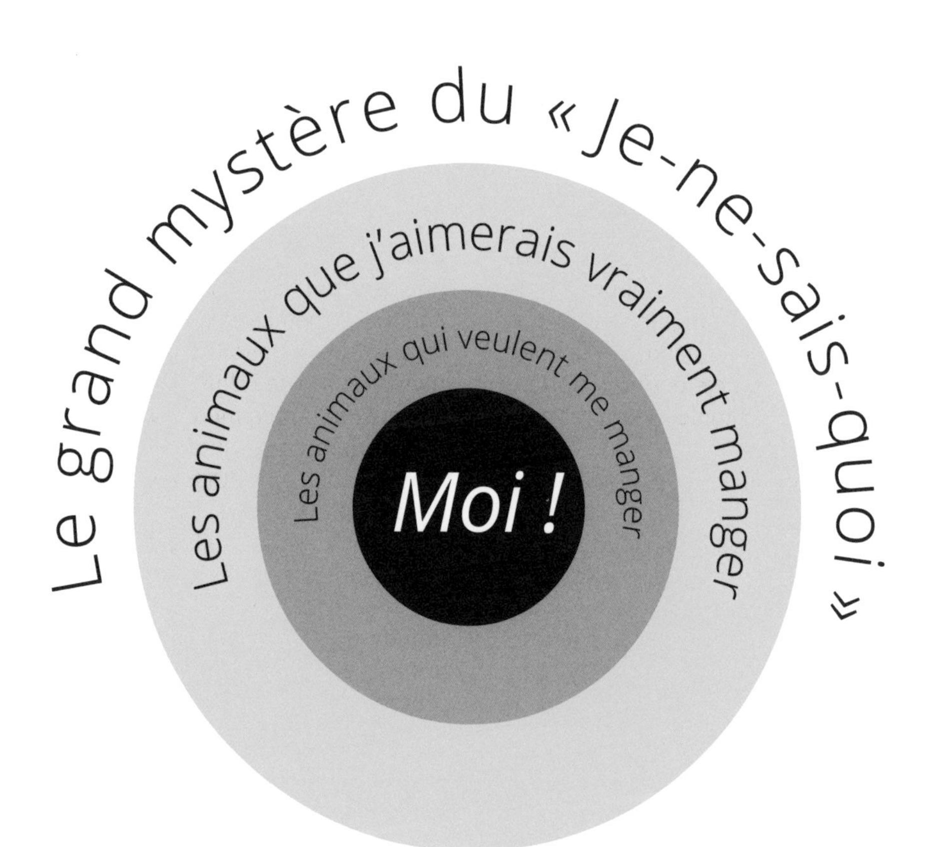

LE MONDE VU PAR LES GRECS ANCIENS

Puis les hommes politiques ont pris la relève. Comme ils avaient réponse à tout, ils étaient capables d'expliquer même les catastrophes naturelles : les coupables étaient les tribus voisines, qui adoraient des dieux vicieux. Et quand ils déclaraient la guerre, c'était au nom de leur soi-disant supériorité culturelle. C'est ainsi que les campagnes militaires animées par l'égoïsme pouvaient passer pour des missions altruistes dont le but était de civiliser des barbares sauvages bien avant l'époque de George W. Bush.

Les Grecs anciens considéraient leur civilisation comme l'apogée du progrès humain, les autres peuples n'étant que des simples témoins de leur supériorité. Leur élitisme n'a pas été affaibli par leur contact avec d'autres sociétés florissantes, bien au contraire. Ils ont emprunté son alphabet à la Phénicie, et l'Égypte leur a appris à construire des temples capables de résister aux tremblements de terre pendant des siècles.

Puisque l'arrogance culturelle perdure en dépit de tous les arguments qui essaient de l'éroder, imaginez la situation en Extrême-Orient, quand l'ancien Empire chinois s'est unifié avec une précision géométrique autour de son centre géographique sans être inquiété par les puissances étrangères. Il n'y avait pas de mer Méditerranée pour séparer le pays en deux, pas d'îles minuscules pour abriter des dissidents prêts à prêcher la désobéissance auprès d'adolescents frustrés. L'emprise de l'empereur était à la fois matérielle et spirituelle. Avec son œil-qui-voit-tout et son pouvoir absolu, c'était un dieu. Et si Sa Divine Majesté éternuait, la Chine tout entière s'enrhumait, histoire de respecter le sacro-saint protocole.

Cette géométrie politique était si parfaite qu'elle n'avait pas besoin d'inventer des histoires pour expliquer l'origine des barbares qui en étaient exclus. Là où les Grecs anciens avaient recours à la mythologie, les Chinois se contentaient de manier la prose.

Ils parlaient tout simplement des barbares du Nord, du Sud, de ceux d'Orient ou d'Occident.

Cette superposition des données spirituelles et géographiques apparaît dans la plupart des cartes de l'Europe médiévale qu'on peut voir aujourd'hui. Étant donné la complexité historique de l'Europe, elles nous semblent délicieusement pittoresques. Loin de se contenter de guider les navigateurs, des chefs-d'œuvre tels que les cartes de Hereford et d'Ebstorf (XIIIe siècle) regroupent mythologie, religion, géographie et histoire dans un collage encyclopédique. Jérusalem y est au centre, et le trône de Jésus au sommet.

On y trouve aussi une variété de stéréotypes, préjugés et autres hallucinations, tous dessinés et annotés. Le portrait du monde chrétien avec ses lieux saints y côtoie les concepts grecs d'après lesquels les extrémités de la terre seraient peuplées de mutants dont les particularités physiques sont dues aux conditions climatiques qu'ils subissent.

Ceci montre que même au temps de la Grèce antique, on ne se préoccupait pas de vérifier les faits. Pas plus qu'au Moyen-Âge, dont voici quelques élucubrations :

C'est en Extrême-Orient que vit la tribu du Yeti, dont les disciples font preuve d'ingéniosité : quand ils sont couchés, leurs pieds sont tellement grands qu'ils leur servent de parasols, réduisant ainsi les risques de mélanome. L'Afrique est peuplée de cyclopes et de créatures à quatre yeux, dont il faut probablement rechercher l'origine dans un ancien laboratoire spécialisé en greffe oculaire. Les fils de Caïn hantent les terres gelées de Sibérie. Exilés par Alexandre le Grand, ils attendent leur heure en rêvant de massacre vengeurs.

Mais le pays le plus intéressant est la Scandinavie du Nord, peuplée d'hommes à tête de chien. On ne sait pas bien si ces créatures existent vraiment, mais le problème qui les entoure est d'ordre théologique : ont-ils une âme ? et si on les convertissait au christianisme, pourraient-ils être sauvés ? Voilà ce qui préoccupait et divisait les érudits du Moyen-Âge.

Ces monstres nous font sourire aujourd'hui, mais comment imaginer que les gens y croyaient vraiment ? Une telle naïveté fait frémir.

Notre monde est cerné par la technologie, qui n'autorise pas l'improvisation. Quant aux préjugés, qui s'articulent autour de mythes et de croyances, pourquoi résistent-ils ?

LE MONDE VU PAR LA CHINE ANCIENNE

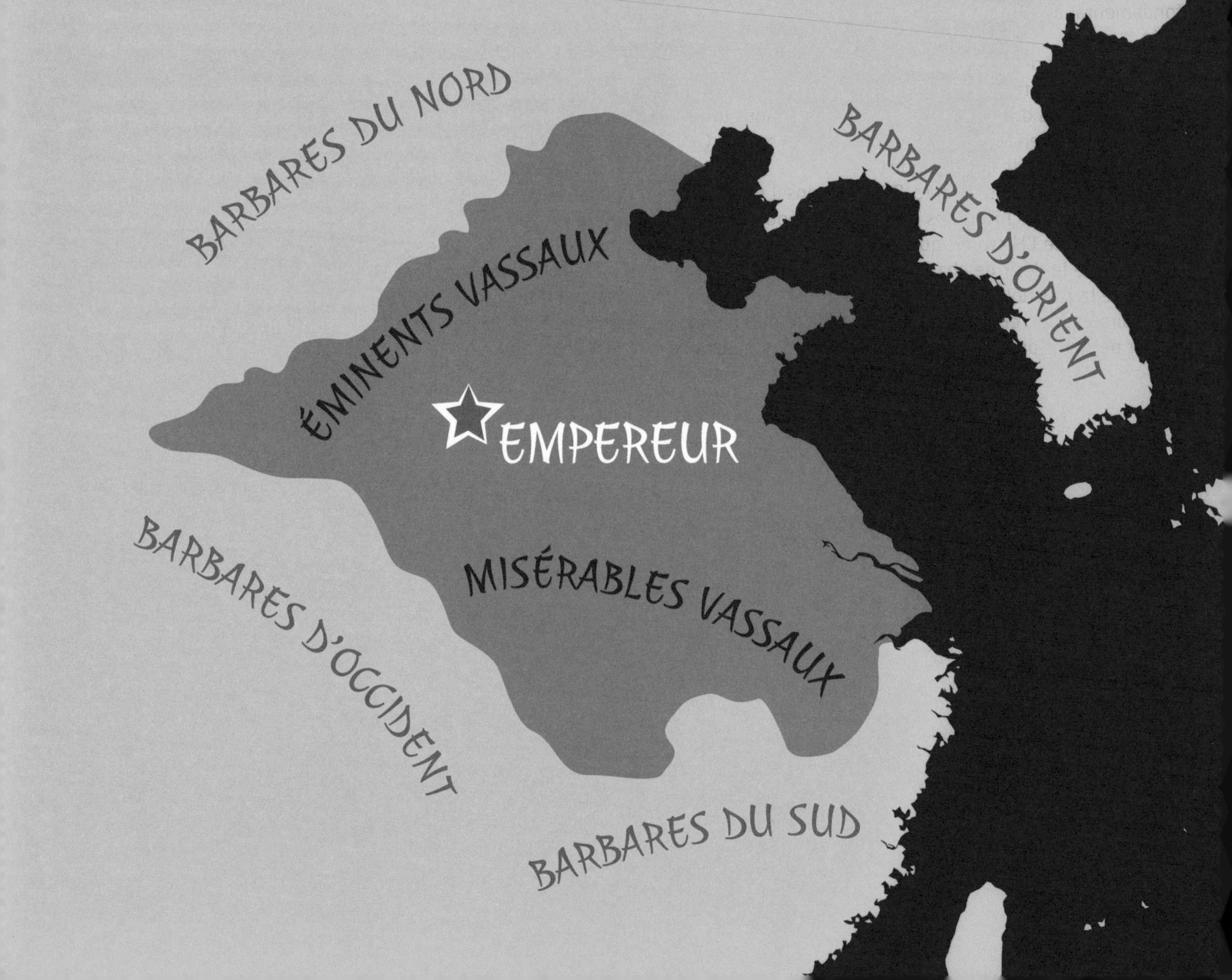

BARBARES DU NORD

BARBARES D'ORIENT

ÉMINENTS VASSAUX

EMPEREUR

MISÉRABLES VASSAUX

BARBARES D'OCCIDENT

BARBARES DU SUD

Inhérents à la nature humaine, ils lui sont indispensables. Et pourtant, la notion d'utilité évolue et ce que l'on jugeait inévitable hier peut se révéler superflu. Ce qui semble universel et fondamental aujourd'hui deviendra sans doute superficiel demain.

Pour les pères de la démocratie athénienne, l'esclavage était une composante essentielle de la société. Et cette réalité, nous essayons de l'ignorer chaque fois que nous louons la Grèce antique, berceau de la civilisation occidentale. Quel bel exemple d'amnésie idéologique !

L'esprit humain est insondable. Pour certains il est figé car incapable de s'affranchir de ses erreurs. Que répondre à leur pessimisme ? Que l'Histoire, qui se répète, leur donne raison... mais que le désir de changement appartient plutôt au domaine de la psychologie.

L'Histoire est une étrange créature. Elle a le don de nous aveugler de notre propre reflet quand nous nous penchons vers ses eaux profondes et mystérieuses. Beaucoup d'entre nous s'y noient, comme Narcisse dont la fascination pour sa propre beauté était plus forte que son instinct de survie. Ceux qui ne connaissent pas l'Histoire seront peut-être condamnés à la répéter. De même que ceux qui la connaissent mais qui l'interprètent comme ça les arrange.

Laissons ce côté inéluctable, et sollicitons davantage notre cerveau, cela nous aidera à nous dépouiller de nos préjugés. Si nous rejetons le prêt-à-penser ressassé dans toutes les manifestations de relations publiques et les campagnes de pub, et si nous assumons nos propres choix, nous éviterons de juger à la hâte et, j'en suis sûr, nous vivrons mieux.

Dans ce monde interconnecté, où l'information se répand plus vite que la pensée, les préjugés ne sont peut-être rien d'autre qu'un effet secondaire de notre paresse intellectuelle.

HOMMES À TÊTE DE CHIEN
SINGES
Femmes suceuses de sang
DÉVOREU
DE FŒTU
EUROPE
BUFFLES
ZOMBIES AFFAMÉS
CRÉATURES AUX YEUX GRIS
AMAZO
ROME
CONSTANTINOPLE
BISONS
ASIE
GRIFFONS
LES ÎLES FORTUNÉES
CRÉATURES RAMPANTES
FOURMIS GÉANTES
CENTAURES
JÉRUSALEM
BÊTE MOITIÉ COQ MOITIÉ SERPENT
LICORNES
AFRIQUE
CYCLOPES
HERMAPHRODITES
CRÉATURES AVEC LES YEUX SUR LES SEINS
PHOENIX
CRÉATURES À QUATRE YEUX
CRÉATURES SANS BOUCHE

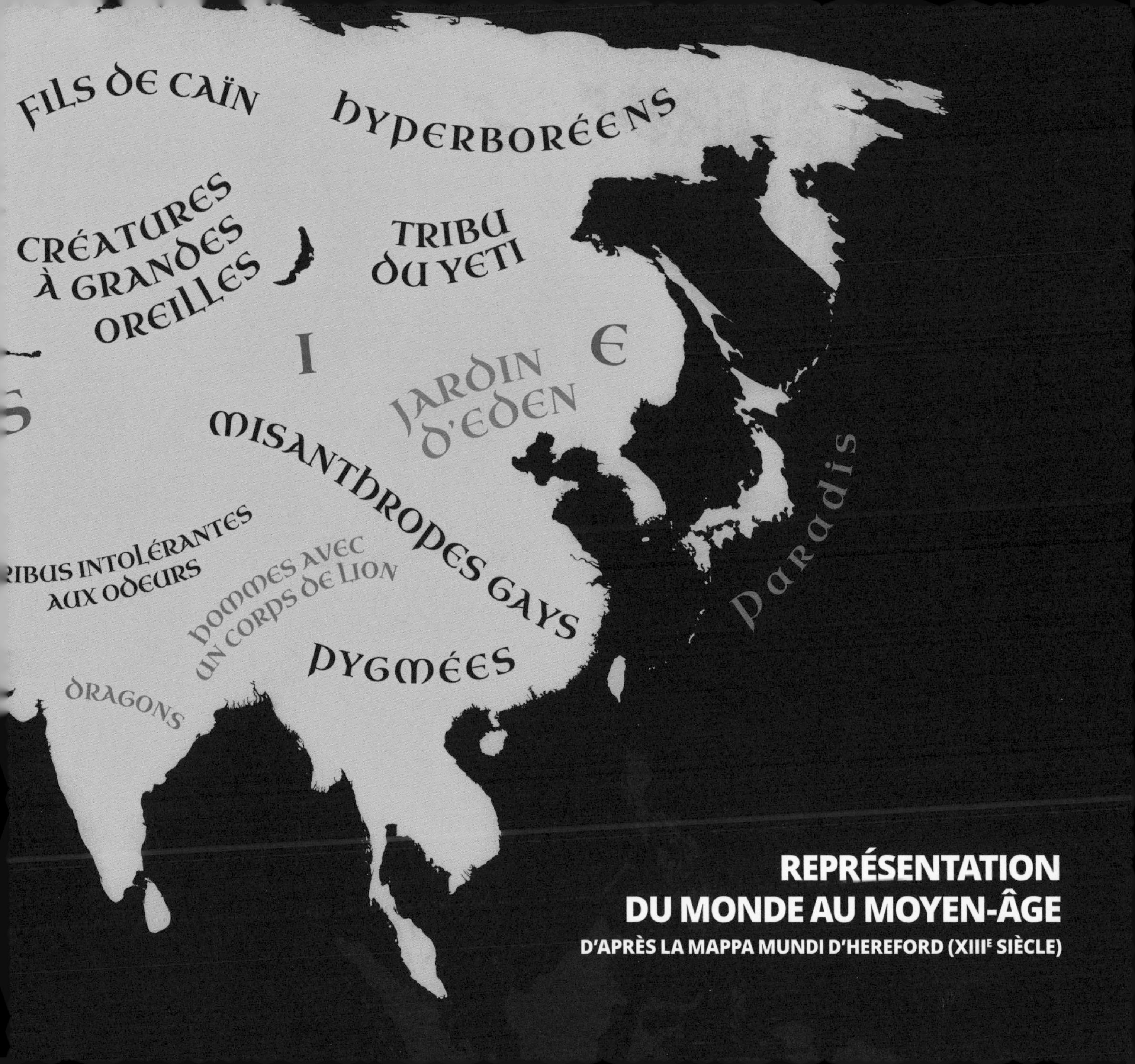

REPRÉSENTATION DU MONDE AU MOYEN-ÂGE

D'APRÈS LA MAPPA MUNDI D'HEREFORD (XIIIE SIÈCLE)

FILS DE CAÏN
HYPERBORÉENS
CRÉATURES À GRANDES OREILLES
TRIBU DU YETI
S I E
JARDIN D'EDEN
MISANTHROPES GAYS
RIBUS INTOLÉRANTES AUX ODEURS
HOMMES AVEC UN CORPS DE LION
PYGMÉES
DRAGONS
Paradis

L'ÂGE EUROPÉEN DE L'INCESTE

Il n'y avait pas d'iPhones au Moyen-Âge, personne ne dira le contraire. Nous avons tous conscience de cet immense fossé technologique qui s'est creusé depuis la période médiévale. Mais les différences politiques qui l'ont accompagné me semblent plus difficiles à définir. La plus importante concerne le concept de nation qui ne correspondait à rien au Moyen-Âge. Il a fallu attendre le XVIIe siècle et la guerre de Trente Ans pour que naisse l'idée d'un état national.

Dans l'Europe du XVIe siècle, les États appartenaient à des aristocrates, eux-mêmes associés à un roi ou une reine. Des régions entières changeaient de propriétaire aussi souvent qu'Imelda Marcos changeait de chaussures. Les mariages royaux étaient des actes politiques qui consolidaient ou divisaient des empires. Comme les aristocrates influents ne voulaient pas partager leur pouvoir avec des inconnus, ils se mariaient entre cousins. C'est ainsi que les fortunes ont prospéré… et que les désordres génétiques s'en sont suivis.

Parmi les monarques européens les plus puissants, citons *Charles Quint, par la grâce de dieu, Empereur du Saint-Empire Romain, toujours Auguste, Roi de Germanie, Roi d'Italie, Roi des Espagnes, de Castille, d'Aragon, de Leòn, de Navarre, de Grenade, de Tolède, de Valence, de Galice, de Majorque, de Séville, de Cordoue, de Murcie, de Jaen, des Algarves, d'Algésiras, de Gibraltar, des îles Canaries, Roi des Deux-Siciles, de Sardaigne, de Corse, Roi de Jérusalem, Roi des Indes Occidentales et Orientales, Roi des îles et de la mer Océane, Archiduc d'Autriche, Duc de Bourgogne, du Brabant, de Lorraine, de Styrie, de Carinthie, de Carniole, de Limbourg, de Luxembourg, de Gueldre, de Néopatrie, de Würtemberg, Landgrave d'Alsace, Prince de Souabe, des Asturies et de Catalogne, Comte de Flandres, de Habsbourg, du Tyrol, de Gorizia, de Barcelone, d'Artois, du Palatinat de Bourgogne, de Hainaut, de Hollande, de Seeland, de Ferrette, de Kyburg, de Namur, de Roussillon, de Cerdagne, de Drenthe, de Zutphen, Margravec du Saint-Empire Romain Germanique, Marquis de Burgau, d'Oristano et de Gociano, Lord de Frise, des cités Baltes* (celles-ci étaient dans la zone Wende, qui regroupe Poméranie, Mecklembourg et Brandebourg), *de Pordenone, de Biscaye, Molins, Salins, Tripoli et Malines*, fruit de siècles d'incestes royaux.

En conséquence, il souffrait d'un prognathisme mandibulaire prononcé. Ce désordre génétique, qui se traduit par une position fortement avancée du menton, s'est répandu dans sa dynastie sous l'appellation de « mâchoire des Habsbourg ».

Comme il avait du mal à mâcher correctement, il avait des problèmes de digestion et il prenait habituellement ses repas seul. La logique veut que de tels défauts génétiques signifiaient également abondance de biens et de territoires.

L'EUROPE D'APRÈS CHARLES QUINT 1555

On lui attribue ces propos célèbres : « Je parle espagnol avec Dieu, italien avec les femmes, français avec les hommes, et allemand avec mon cheval. » Non contentes de nous rappeler qu'au début du XVe siècle les chevaux étaient bons en allemand, ses paroles montrent l'esprit cosmopolite de Sa Majesté.

Charles Quint régnait sur un empire colonial immense doté de richesses colossales. Novateur en matière de fiscalité, il a emprunté aux banquiers génois pour financer ses guerres et chasser les Français d'Italie. Vaincus, ceux-ci sont repartis en emmenant avec eux Léonard de Vinci, qui fut séduit par François Ier.

Voilà peut-être pourquoi la Joconde est aujourd'hui au Louvre, mais n'en tenez pas rigueur à Charles Quint. Personne n'aurait pu prévoir qu'un portrait banal d'une femme à la beauté discutable deviendrait un jour le tableau le plus célèbre du monde.

François Ier était l'ennemi juré de Charles Quint. Non content de sa victoire à Marignan, le roi de France eut recours à des mesures extrêmes en s'alliant avec la seule personne qui puisse rivaliser avec l'empereur : Soliman le Magnifique, sultan de l'Empire ottoman.

C'était la première fois qu'un roi chrétien s'unissait à une puissance musulmane. À deux reprises Soliman assiégea Vienne, faisant ainsi des ravages dans le monde catholique. À son départ, il oublia quelques sacs de café et un panier de croissants. Les Autrichiens, séduits, s'emparèrent de la recette. Celle-ci fut ensuite volée par les Français... qui sont persuadés qu'elle appartient à leur héritage culturel.

LA GRAND-MÈRE RONCHON DE L'EUROPE

L'Histoire de l'Autriche est vraiment étonnante. Comment imaginer qu'il y a cent ans ce petit pays était le plus grand empire du continent (si on exclut la Russie impériale) ? Les Habsbourg étaient presque arrivés à faire de l'Europe une grande entité politique, bien avant que Napoléon puis Hitler n'essaient d'imposer leur empire continental ou que l'Union européenne ne réadapte l'idée d'une intégration économique et politique.

La configuration finale de l'empire – la double monarchie d'Autriche-Hongrie – s'est désintégrée de façon dramatique dans le tourbillon de la Première Guerre mondiale, alors que les mouvements nationalistes émergeaient sur tout le continent. On associe habituellement cette guerre à la Révolution russe en oubliant de mentionner la désintégration de l'Autriche-Hongrie, qui fut un évènement extrêmement dramatique. En une nuit, Vienne, qui était au centre de la puissance européenne, est devenue une ville de province comme une autre. Elle a tout perdu, sauf sa beauté et ses musées. Et tout comme Saint-Pétersbourg, elle ne s'est jamais remise de ce cataclysme.

La monarchie s'est effondrée parce qu'elle a été incapable de se réformer. En plus de sa complexité ethnique, ses dirigeants souffraient de myopie idéologique : plutôt que de faire face à la modernité, ils ne faisaient que s'encombrer des traditions qu'ils voulaient préserver. Pour Klemens von Metternich, le plus célèbre des politiciens autrichiens du XIXe siècle, l'essor de la liberté de la presse était le pire de tous les maux. Pourtant, il n'avait rien d'un dictateur parano qui prendrait plaisir à manipuler les foules. Il pensait seulement que le public n'était pas suffisamment qualifié pour comprendre quelque chose à l'art de gouverner.

Le début de la Première Guerre mondiale est un drame qui n'est pas sans rappeler la légende de Troie. Comme l'histoire d'Hélène, il transforme un problème banalement politique en une tragédie grecque à part entière, dans laquelle même les dieux ressemblent à des marionnettes.

En 1914, l'archiduc et prince héritier François-Ferdinand était en visite à Sarajevo : l'Autriche-Hongrie venait d'annexer officiellement la Bosnie, mosaïque dont chaque élément était incompatible avec la culture autrichienne. Les conseillers de François-Ferdinand savaient probablement que des militaires serbes, qui voyaient dans cette annexion un acte de guerre, fomentaient son assassinat. Mais, fidèle au mépris traditionnel de la réalité, l'archiduc préféra minimiser le danger et circuler en ville dans une voiture découverte, sa femme Sophie à ses côtés.

L'EUROPE VUE PAR L'AUTRICHE-HONGRIE 1914

Bien que duchesse, cette dernière était traitée comme une roturière par la Cour d'Autriche, sans doute parce qu'elle était d'origine tchèque. On comprend peut-être mieux le désir du jeune couple de s'amuser loin de Vienne, loin du vieil empereur grincheux.

Cet assassinat ne fut pas un travail d'amateur. Ils étaient quatre à suivre le cortège de voitures. Les deux premiers n'ont rien pu faire, mais le troisième lança une bombe sur la voiture de l'archiduc. Le hasard fait qu'elle a rebondi avant d'exploser sous une autre voiture, blessant plusieurs personnes.

L'archiduc arriva sain et sauf à l'hôtel de ville puis il se rendit à l'hôpital pour y visiter les victimes de l'attentat raté. Au retour, on changea d'itinéraire pour éviter le centre-ville, mais le chauffeur prit une décision fatale : il arrêta la voiture archiducale juste en face du quatrième larron, Gavrilo Princip. Cette fois-ci, l'assassin ne manqua pas sa cible.

Ceci conduisit à une déclaration de guerre contre la Serbie. Puisque les deux pays appartenaient à des camps opposés et que leurs alliés étaient obligés de les soutenir militairement, le continent tout entier est devenu un immense abattoir.

L'EUROPE CONTEMPORAINE

Bien que j'évite systématiquement les pièges à touristes, je finis toujours par grimper au sommet d'une tour pour avoir une vue panoramique de la ville que je visite. Tout ça pour faire plaisir à un copain qui me traîne là-haut sous prétexte de me prendre en photo. Comme s'il ne savait pas que je déteste faire comme tout le monde.

Je me souviens de mon premier séjour à Rome : à peine arrivé, j'étais déjà au sommet de la basilique Saint-Pierre. La vue n'était pas inintéressante, mais je n'ai pas été très emballé car une ville vue d'en haut ne m'a jamais fasciné.

Ce qui m'a impressionné ce jour-là, ce sont les toilettes publiques au sommet, juste en dessous du dôme. Ce fut une belle découverte car lorsqu'on décide d'arpenter Rome, trouver un endroit pour faire pipi relève du défi.

Quelques années plus tard, il m'a fallu grimper au sommet de la tour de Galata à Istamboul. Je l'ai fait sans mérite : j'ai utilisé l'ascenseur. Et une fois là-haut je me suis laissé aller à faire quelques photos.

Soudain, j'ai eu une révélation. J'avais sous les yeux le début de l'Europe. À un kilomètre de là, dans cette même ville, divisée par les eaux bleues du Bosphore, c'était l'Asie. J'ai trouvé ça remarquable : il n'y avait rien de différent, les immeubles étaient les mêmes, ceux qui y habitaient étaient les mêmes, ils parlaient la même langue, ils vivaient dans la même ville, mais celle-ci était écartelée entre deux continents.

Écartelée n'est pas le mot qui convient. Berlin a été écartelée. C'est une ville où se sont affrontés deux mondes. On ne pouvait pas aller de l'un à l'autre sans risquer de se faire tirer dessus. Istamboul est tellement différente, avec ses deux ponts et ses centaines de bateaux qui vous font traverser. Il n'y a pas de mur. Le détroit est une autoroute. Au XVIIe siècle un certain Hezârfen Ahmed Çelebi est même parvenu à s'élancer de la tour de Galata et à planer jusqu'à Dogancilar sur la rive asiatique du Bosphore, grâce aux ailes qu'il s'était confectionnées.

Celui qui a choisi cet endroit pour en faire la frontière entre l'Europe et l'Asie était un imbécile. Il n'y a aucune raison, qu'elle soit géographique, historique ou culturelle pour installer une frontière sur une rivière qui traverse une ville. Laquelle ville a été la métropole européenne la plus puissante pendant plus de mille ans...

Istamboul est tout sauf un signe de ponctuation. De part sa situation, une ville comme Lisbonne conviendrait davantage : elle seule permet de commencer une phrase, ou de la terminer.

Quand, du sommet de la tour Belém, vous regardez l'océan Atlantique, vous ressentez un vide étrange. Lisbonne est restée accrochée à l'extrémité du monde pendant qu'Istamboul en occupait le centre. En face, il n'y avait rien et seule la mythologie peuplait le néant. Le jardin des Hespérides, les îles mystérieuses d'Antillia et Thulé, l'Atlantide engloutie, se cachaient plus loin que l'horizon, et seule l'imagination des rêveurs et des poètes leur donnait vie.

Mais aujourd'hui Lisbonne a changé. Il est loin, le temps de l'expansion de l'empire colonial portugais, qui s'étendait de l'Amazonie aux confins de l'Indonésie.

On peut peut-être placer les limites de l'Europe au nord là où l'Islande est située, sur la dorsale médio-atlantique qui sépare les plaques tectoniques d'Amérique et d'Europe. Mais même cette limite n'est pas précise car, à l'ouest, se trouve le Canada...dont la reine vit à Londres. Alors qui peut dire où commence et où finit l'Europe ?

Un Britannique vous dira qu'elle commence à Calais et qu'elle finit quelque part dans les marais de Finlande. Et, comme la plupart de ses compatriotes, il en exclura la Russie bien que sa superficie couvre le tiers du continent. Je ne pense pas que les Russes apprécieraient. Ils vous rappelleraient que leur pays a une frontière commune avec la Corée du Nord et qu'il n'est ni européen ni asiatique mais simplement russe. Un habitant d'Amérique latine verrait probablement dans les Européens des impérialistes qui ont envahi le Nouveau Monde pour y détruire les cultures indigènes. Même si plus de la moitié des pays du Vieux Continent n'avaient pas de colonies, même si certains étaient occupés, divisés ou dirigés par des étrangers.

Lors d'une visite à Cordoue, en Espagne, j'ai vu une pancarte dans une rue : « S'il vous plaît, faites comme les Européens, ne touchez pas les fleurs ! » J'ai entendu ce genre de message dans ma Bulgarie natale. Le terme « Européen » y est souvent pris comme une référence à des étrangers plus civilisés que nous, une sorte d'idéal inaccessible auquel personne ne croit mais que tout le monde fait semblant de poursuivre. Parfois, même les Européens ne se sentent pas Européens. Une chose est sûre : l'Europe a autant besoin de frontières que les poissons ont besoin de vélos.

L'EUROPE VUE PAR LA FRANCE
VRAIMENT TROP FROID
PEUPLE HAUTAIN QUI AIME LE FROID
MOUSTIQUES ET BOULETTES DE VIANDE
TÉLÉPHONES MOBILES
LE RÊVE DE NAPOLÉON
BRÛLEURS DE PUCELLE
CATHOLIQUES
VIKINGS
TRIBUS BALTES
RUSSES BLANCS
HERBE
MEILLEURS AMIS
PLOMBIERS
UN PEU LA FRANCE
ANTI-EUROPÉENS
C'ÉTAIT PAS L'URSS, ICI ?
SLAVES
FRANCE
VIEIL ENNEMI
SARKOLAND
COUSINS PAUVRES
UN PEU LA FRANCE
FRÈRES PAUVRES
TERRA INCOGNITA
PRESQUE FRANÇAIS
SAUVAGES PAUVRES
ALLIÉS DES ANGLAIS
VACANCES PAS CHÈRES
BRUYANTS ET POILUS
PAS PRÈS D'ÊTRE EUROPÉENS
TOUJOURS UN PEU LA FRANCE

L'EUROPE VUE PAR LA GRANDE-BRETAGNE

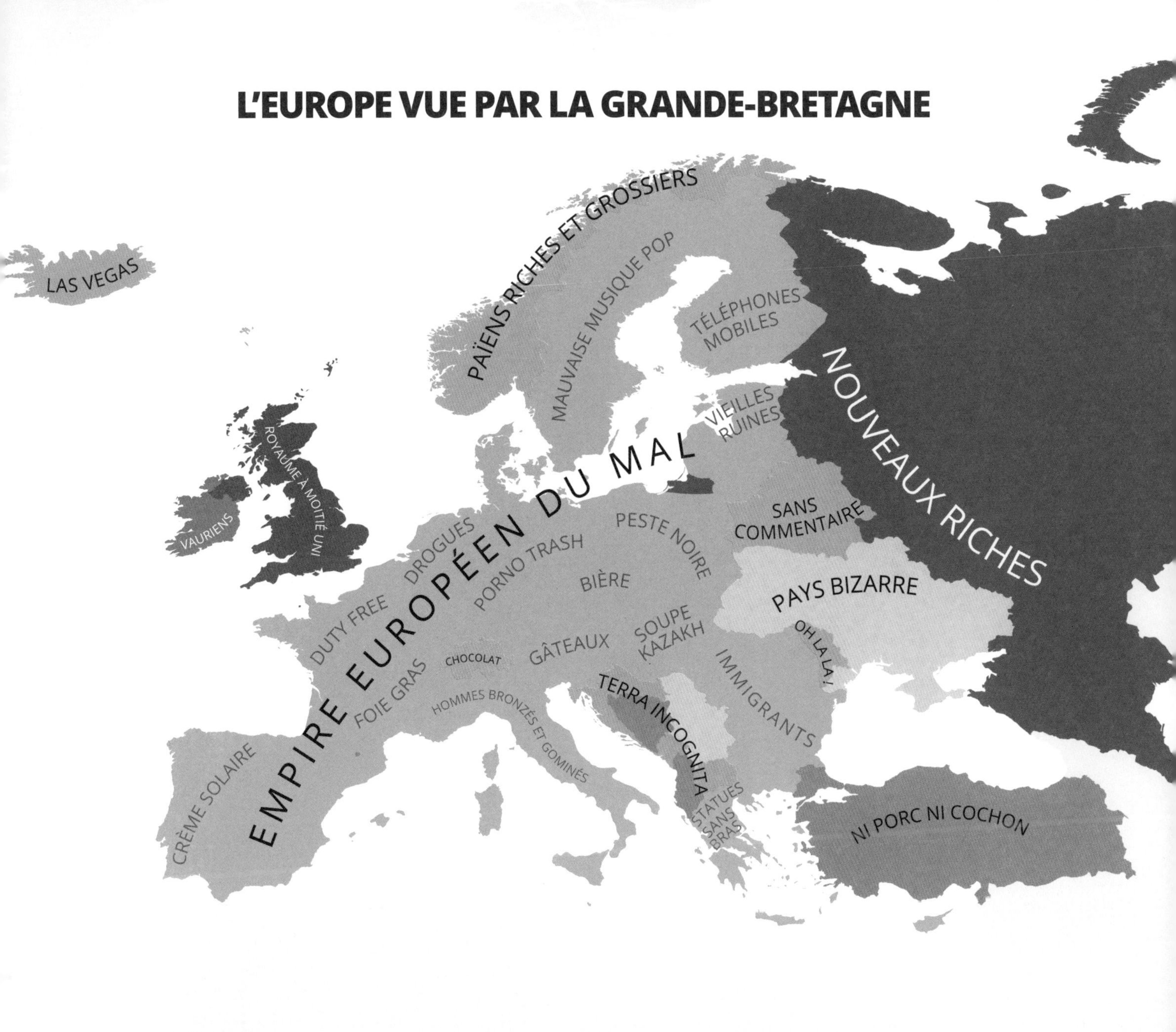

L'EUROPE VUE PAR L'ALLEMAGNE

L'EUROPE VUE PAR LA GRÈCE

L'EUROPE VUE PAR L'ITALIE

L'EUROPE VUE PAR LA RUSSIE

L'EUROPE VUE PAR LA SUISSE

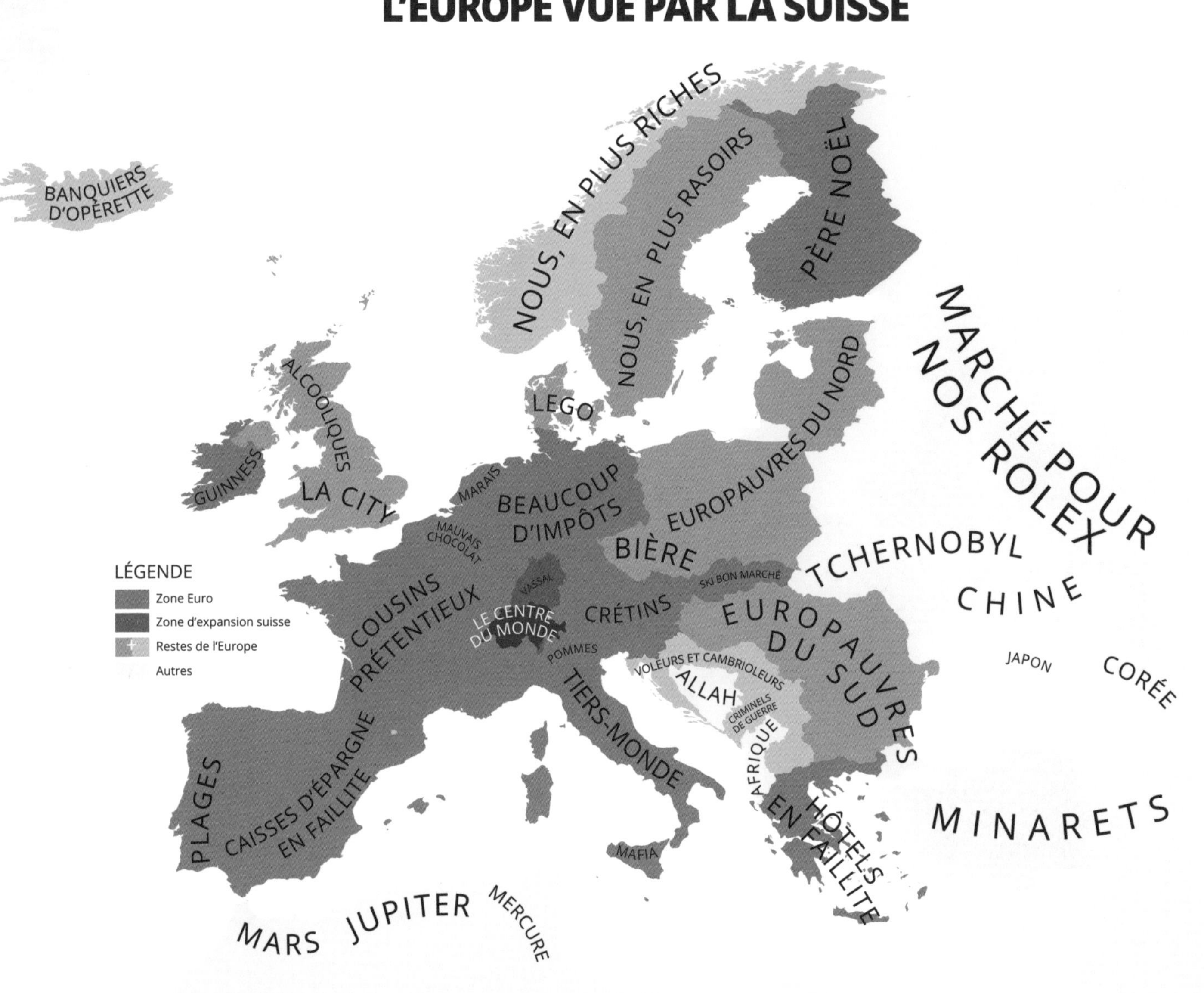

L'EUROPE VUE PAR LE VATICAN

L'EUROPE VUE PAR LA TURQUIE
GEYSERS HAMMAMS
ARABIE SAOUDITE DU NORD
MOBILIER NON TURC
VRAIES BLONDES
FILLES SEXY
TROP DÉPRIMANTS
JYLLANDS-POSTEN
TROP DE BACON
IVROGNES
FAUSSES TULIPES
BUREAU-CRATES
RÉPUBLIQUE DU KHEBAB DE TURQUIE DU NORD
TERRE DE PASSION
BLANCS DÉGÉNÉRÉS
BORDELS
SKODA
ON A FAILLI LES BATTRE
1683
GOULASH
TIERS-MONDE
GITANS
BOUFFEURS DE CROISSANTS HYPOCRITES
MARGINAUX
SLAVES ITALIENS
CRIMINELS
TERRORISTES
ENCORE À NOUS
MAFIA
OUI!
VOISINS BIPOLAIRES
FOUS
COUSINS
VOYOUS
ANATOLIE ROMAINE
TURQUIE EUROPÉENNE
(pour mémoire, c'est plus grand que Chypre, Malte et le Luxembourg)
LANCEURS DE COUTEAUX
RÂLEURS
TURQUIE
ORANGES
TROP DE PORC
CHYPRE LIBRE
CHYPRE OCCUPÉE PAR L'UE
VOLÉ PAR LES FRANÇAIS
KURDES ET MCDONALD'S

L'EUROPE VUE PAR LA POLOGNE

L'EUROPE VUE PAR L'AUTRICHE

L'EUROPE VUE PAR LA BULGARIE

L'EUROPE VUE PAR L'ESPAGNE

LA PÉNINSULE IBÉRIQUE VUE PAR L'ESPAGNE

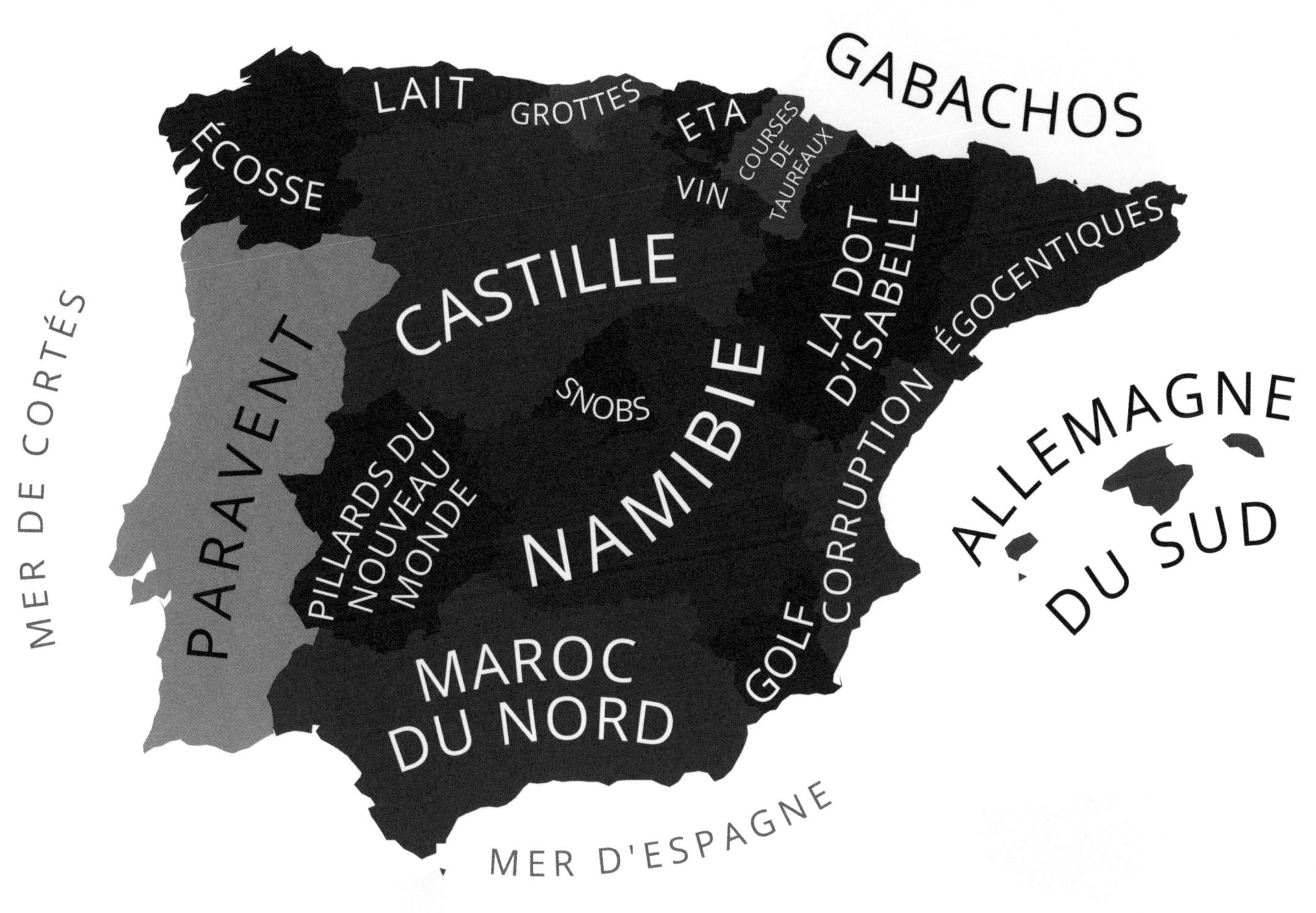

L'EUROPE VUE PAR LES LATINO-AMÉRICAINS

L'EUROPE VUE PAR LES GAYS
CHANTEURS HYPE
ENNUI
MUSIQUE DANCE TRASH
MOUSTIQUES
KILTS
SAUNAS
XXL
?
DÉNI TOTAL
COOL
HASH
PAUVRES MAIS SEXY
DONJON
GAUFFRES
CEINTURE DE CHASTETÉ
DANGEREUX HOMOPHOBES
BIÈRE CHIC
PORNO MILITAIRE
PÂTISSERIE TRÈS CALORIQUE
PORNO NON MILITAIRE
CENTRE COMMERCIAL
EMPIRE DU MARAIS
NEIGE
F.E.V.
TRIBUS HOMOPHOBES
HOMOS HÉTÉROS
OURS
DANCELONA
F.E.V.
HOMMES SEXY ET HOMOPHOBES
FÉDÉRATION DES ÉTATS VACANCIERS (F.E.V.)

LE TOMBEUR EUROPÉEN

Les Français ont Napoléon, les Allemands, Bismarck, les Russes, Staline, et les Juifs, Moïse. Chaque nation a son leader qui incarne son esprit et qui symbolise ses stéréotypes.

S'il y a un personnage qui peut résumer tous les stéréotypes sur les Italiens, c'est bien Silvio Berlusconi. Il est l'emblème d'une culture politique qui a hésité pendant des siècles entre l'excès et la raison.

« Par définition, puisque je suis premier ministre je ne peux pas être un menteur », a-t-il proclamé un jour en s'appropriant l'infaillibilité pontificale. Et il a précisé, inspiré par le modèle des Médicis : « Si, en m'occupant des intérêts d'autrui je m'occupe aussi des miens, on ne peut pas parler de conflit d'intérêts. »

Comment a-t-il pu rester au pouvoir après de telles gaffes médiatiques ? Rappelez-vous comment, accusé d'infidélité, il a essayé de se défendre : il a répondu qu'il valait mieux aimer les jolies filles que d'être gay... Un jeune Italien gay à qui je demandais pourquoi on ne se débarrassait pas d'un tel clown m'a répondu, laconique : « C'est compliqué. »

C'est effectivement compliqué. Il y a eu 60 gouvernements en Italie en 60 ans. Silvio Berlusconi a été à la tête de plusieurs d'entre eux, et a même rempli trois mandats de premier ministre. Le premier, très éphémère, a commencé en 1994 et a duré 8 mois. Le deuxième, pendant lequel il a formé deux gouvernements consécutifs, a commencé en 2001 pour se terminer 4 ans et 11 mois plus tard. Le troisième l'a ramené à la tête de l'État en 2008, pour 3 ans et demi. Cela correspond en tout à plus de 9 ans de pouvoir. Ce n'est pas énorme, mais si on prend en compte l'instabilité qui caractérise la politique de l'après-guerre, une telle longévité ministérielle est un véritable exploit. Si j'étais poète, je dirais qu'elle brille avec plus d'éclat qu'une supernova en train d'exploser.

Ce portrait aide sans doute à comprendre pourquoi il se prenait pour « le Jésus-Christ de la politique », et pourquoi il se disait supérieur à tous les autres, sauf à Napoléon.

Délire de grandeur ? Sens de l'humour déplacé ? Laissons aux biographes et aux psychanalystes le soin de décider. Mais une chose est certaine : c'est l'Italie profonde qui lui a inspiré les provocations les plus impressionnantes.

« Beaucoup d'Italiens le critiquent, m'a dit une femme un jour, mais je ne pense pas qu'ils soient si nombreux que ça. La plupart de ceux qui ne l'apprécient pas sont probablement des gens qui sont partis vivre à l'étranger. Personnellement, je ne l'aime pas, mais ma grand-mère et ma tante l'apprécient, et elles votent toujours pour lui. Ça fait 2 contre 1. Voilà pourquoi il est encore en place. »

L'EUROPE D'APRÈS SILVIO BERLUSCONI
FILLES QUI SENTENT LE POISSON
UNION NORDIQUE DES VRAIES BLONDES
MER DE BALEINES SÉCHÉES
FILLES MÉLANCOLIQUES
HOMMES ENCORE PLUS PETITS QUE MOI
MER DES COUILLONS
FILLES DÉLURÉES
FILLES DE DRUIDES
RÉPUBLIQUE
DÉTROIT DE LA
FLEURS
FILLES DE BUREAUCRATES
FILLES BIEN NOURRIES
FILLES LÉGÈRES
FILLES AUTORITAIRES
FILLES & GAZODUCS
FILLES GRATUITES
PARISIENNES
FILLES RICHES
FILLES CONTRÔLÉES
FILLES À MONOSOURCIL
FILLES PEU CHÈRES
POUBELLE FRANÇAISE DE L'OUEST
FILLES CRIMINELLES
MAMMA MIA
MER CRIMINELLE
MARE DELLE PUTTANE
FILLES EN CHALEUR
FILLES DE PLAGES
POUBELLE FRANÇAISE DU SUD
MER DE LA PASSION
FILLES À GRAND NEZ
FILLES & BAKLAVA
TRÈS ÉTROIT POUR LE MS
SAGA RUBY
MER DES IMMIGRANTS
MER HÉBRAÏQUE

Je trouve excessive l'admiration portée à cet homme qui a toujours confondu business et séduction : d'après lui, si les investisseurs étaient attirés par l'Italie, la beauté des secrétaires y était pour quelque chose. Fidèle à ses soi-disant principes de bonne moralité, il ne précisait jamais quel genre d'affaires on traitait. Mais les révélations sur des « entretiens » avec des prostituées de luxe n'ont plus laissé beaucoup de place à l'imagination.

Un Italien de mes amis essaya de m'éclairer : « C'est pour ça qu'il est populaire. Le public adore son machisme rampant, et les femmes sont véritablement hypnotisées. »

J'avais déjà entendu ça, mais comment admettre que c'était encore valable au XXIe siècle... Et il y a malheureusement d'autres hommes politiques qui usent de tactiques similaires. Bien que leurs cultures soient différentes, leurs comportements se ressemblent. Les affiches qui montrent Poutine torse nu sont l'équivalent russe des propos de Berlusconi sur le rôle des secrétaires. En Bulgarie, le premier ministre, qui a déjà le statut de sex-symbol, joue de son charme à la James Bond pour manipuler les foules.

On dirait qu'en Europe la vénération de l'intelligence vacille au profit d'une adoration plus sensuelle de personnages mythiques. Vous ignorez peut-être comment gérer la crise financière, mais si on voit en vous un type qui sait baiser, présentez-vous aux présidentielles, vous avez toutes les chances d'être élu.

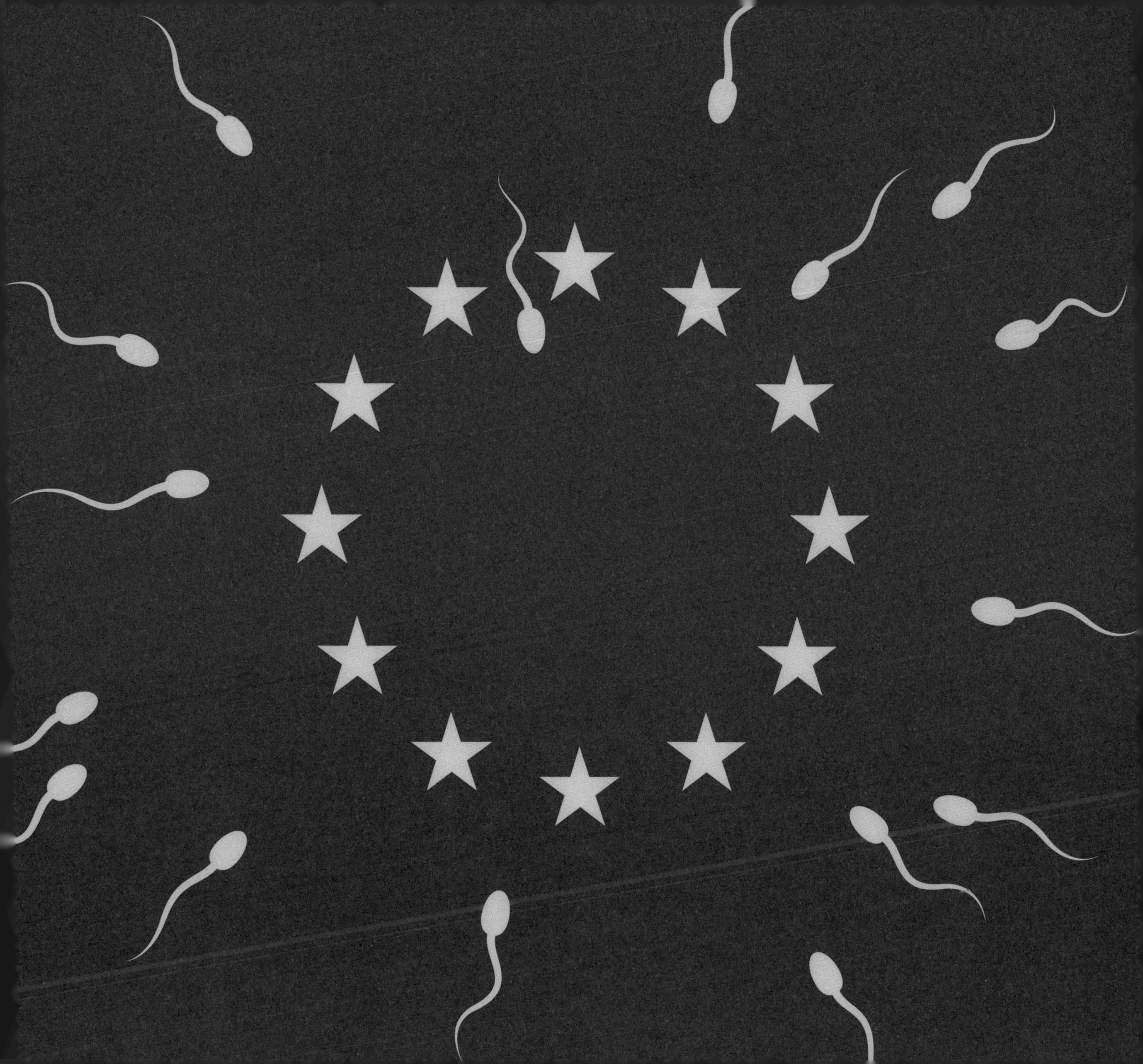

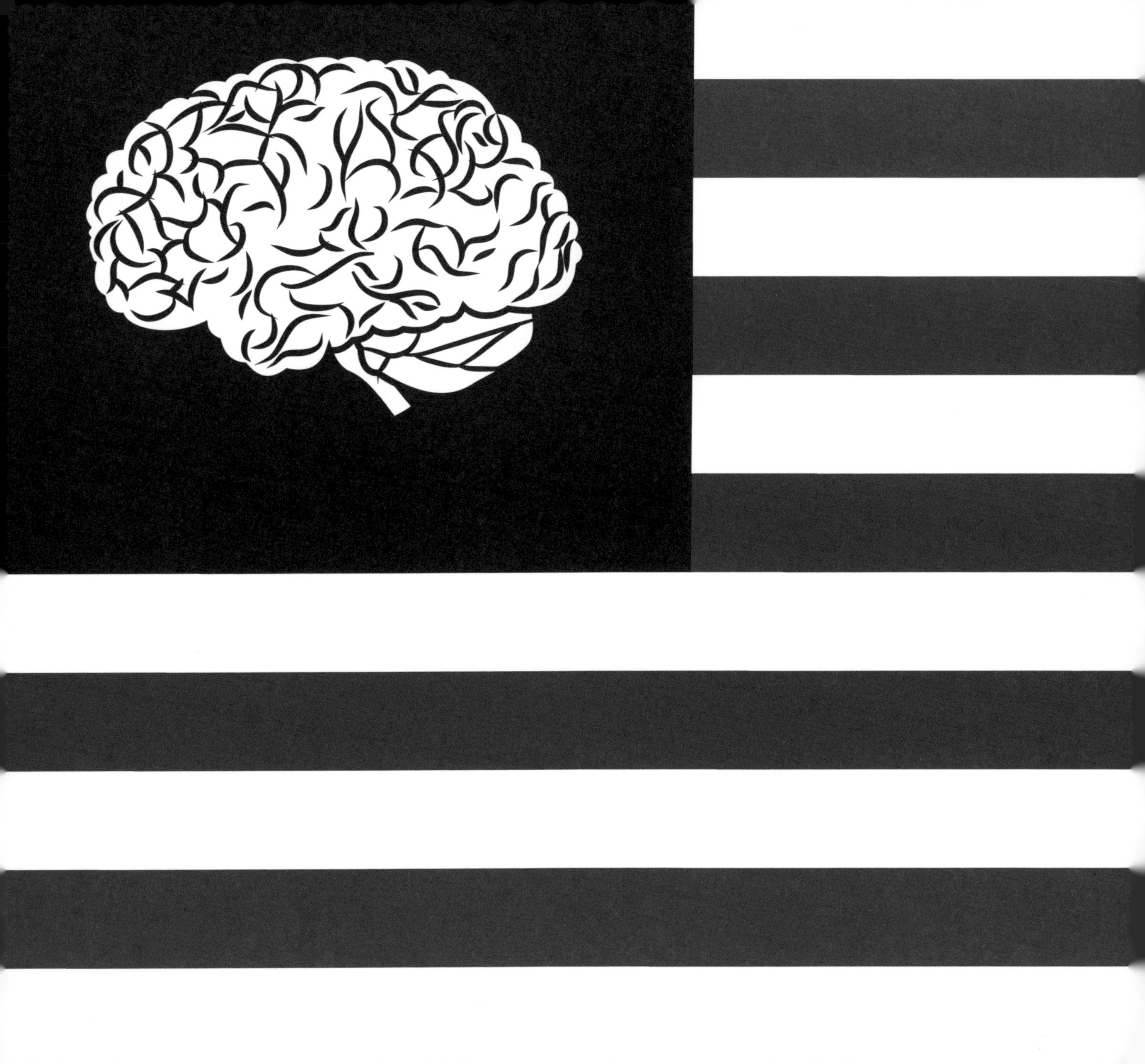

LE MONDE AMÉRICAIN

« Les Américains ont toujours eu le culte de l'ignorance. Cette touche d'anti-intellectualisme, qui a accompagné notre vie politique et culturelle, repose sur un faux principe : la démocratie signifierait que ce que je ne sais pas a autant de valeur que ce que tu sais. »

Cette citation d'Isaac Asimov (« A Cult of Ignorance », *Newsweek*, 21 janvier 1980) est encore d'actualité 32 ans après, et je parie que dans 32 ans elle le sera encore. Car ce qui définit les Américains, ce n'est pas exactement le culte de l'ignorance, c'est plutôt un mépris viscéral pour toute forme d'autorité.

À l'origine, il y a cette croyance que chaque être humain devrait avoir la possibilité de réussir dans la vie, quel que soit son milieu social ou culturel. De tels propos, qui balayaient les différences et qui donnaient une chance à tous, étaient révolutionnaires à l'époque.

En Europe, pour décrire la montée des idées républicaines, nous nous reférons toujours à la Révolution française. En oubliant que celle-ci s'est inspirée de la Révolution américaine, qui a eu lieu 15 ans plus tôt.

Aveuglés par notre supériorité intellectuelle, nous oublions souvent que les idées républicaines ont eu du mal à se répandre sur le Vieux Continent. Comparez les carrières politiques de George Washington et de Napoléon Bonaparte. L'un a été président mais il s'est retiré du pouvoir après deux mandats. L'autre s'est couronné empereur puis il a distribué à sa famille et à ses amis les royaumes qu'il avait conquis.

Ces différences me semblent importantes car elles peuvent engendrer des idées fausses. Un Américain trouverait ridicule d'avoir un monarque héréditaire comme chef d'État, quel que soit le poids du symbole. Pour un Européen qui observe ce qui se passe outre-Atlantique, il est aberrant de pouvoir voter sans présenter aucun document qui prouve votre identité, comme c'est pourtant le cas dans dix-neuf États.

Ces spécificités peuvent sembler un peu caricaturales. Mais le culte de la liberté qui anime les Américains peut être dangereux. Il me fait penser à un feu de camp qu'on aurait oublié d'éteindre. Car la liberté, comme tous les autres idéaux, n'est pas quelque chose qu'on peut définir. Si on arrive à peu près à la codifier en termes politiques et judiciaires, elle échappe à toute définition pour devenir un concept vague, voire contradictoire, quand on l'approche d'un point de vue philosophique et émotionnel.

De plus, la politique repose souvent sur l'émotion alors que la loi s'appuie plutôt sur la philosophie. Une telle disparité ne peut qu'être instable à plus ou moins long terme. « Le prix de la liberté est une vigilance constante » : voilà ce que disait Thomas Jefferson, un autre Père fondateur. Dans ce cas précis, j'aimerais paraphraser ses propos : « Le prix du savoir est une humilité constante. »

C'est ce manque d'humilité qu'Asimov dénonce amèrement. Il définit les pires excès de l'orgueil américain. Il représente le côté le plus sombre de la liberté. Toujours prêt à prendre d'assaut le pays, il revêt des formes différentes pour s'appliquer à toutes sortes de sujets : cela va du débat sur l'avortement à l'opposition bigote aux droits des homosexuels, en passant par la demande ridicule de reconnaissance du créationnisme. Pour terminer par le droit d'être « un imbécile qui n'y connaît rien ».

Parmi les stéréotypes qui caractérisent les Américains, il y a leur « stupidité ». Mais un tel portrait est incorrect car il y a des imbéciles partout dans le monde, dans tous les pays et dans les villages les plus reculés. En général, ces gens-là sont conscients de leurs limites, ils en ont honte. Ils ont tendance à faire profil bas, au moins en ce qui concerne le domaine scientifique. Par contre, en Amérique, l'imbécile est immensément fier de sa propre stupidité. À tel point qu'il peut finir par influencer un discours politique et détourner idéologiquement tout un parti.

L'AMÉRIQUE DU NORD VUE PAR LES USA

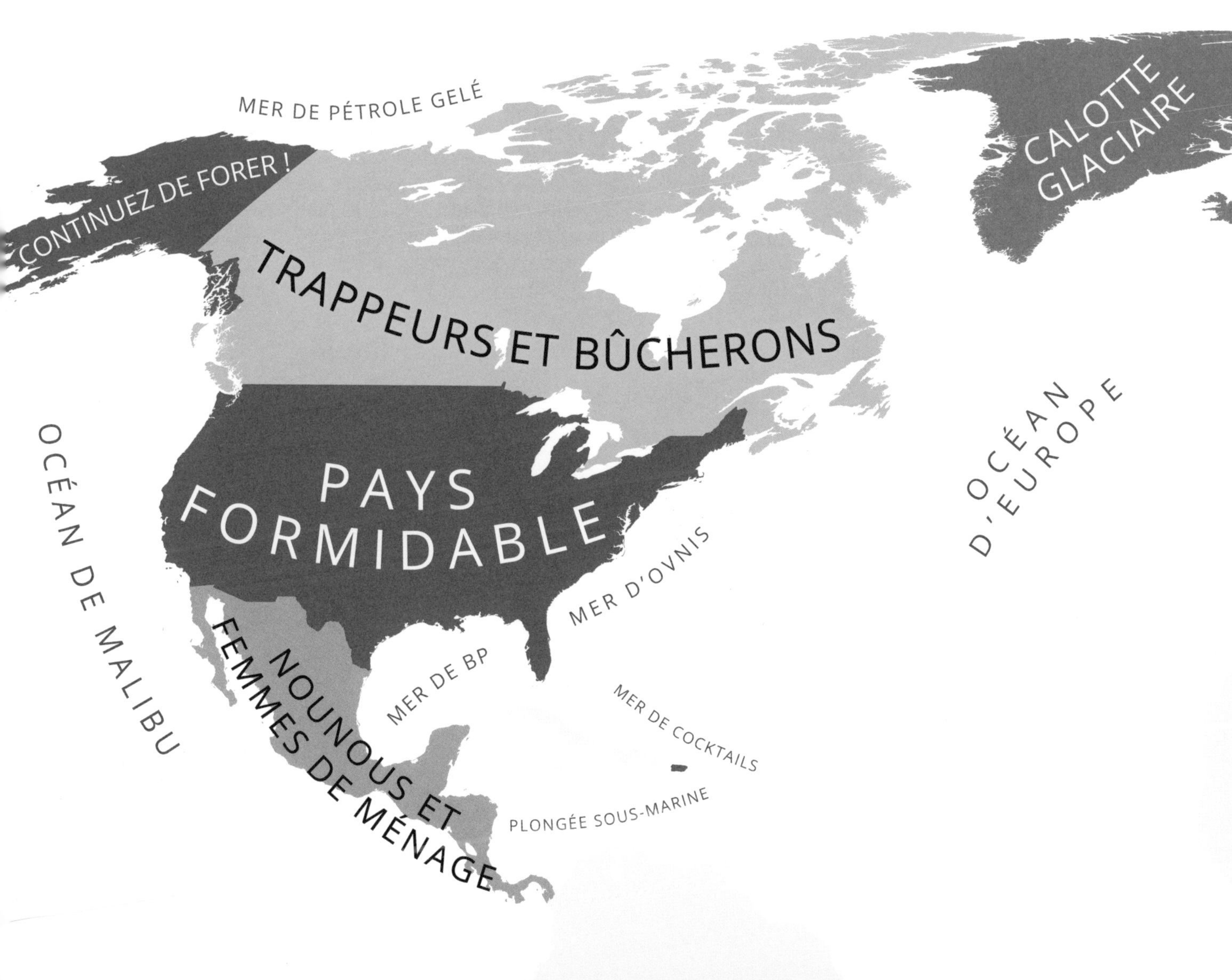

L'EUROPE VUE PAR LES USA

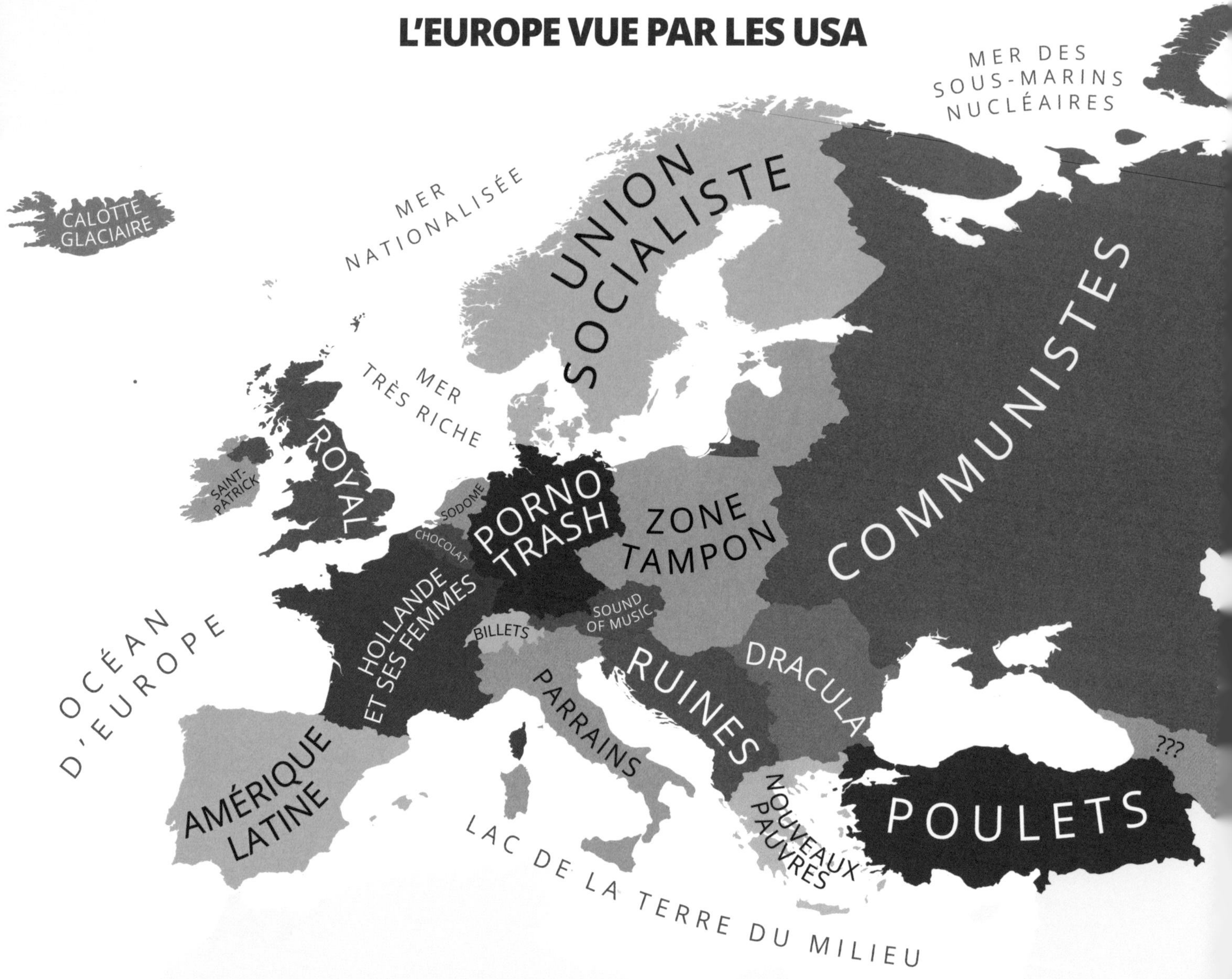

MER DES SOUS-MARINS NUCLÉAIRES
CALOTTE GLACIAIRE
MER NATIONALISÉE
UNION SOCIALISTE
COMMUNISTES
MER TRÈS RICHE
ROYAL
SAINT-PATRICK
SODOME
CHOCOLAT
PORNO TRASH
ZONE TAMPON
HOLLANDE ET SES FEMMES
SOUND OF MUSIC
BILLETS
OCÉAN D'EUROPE
PARRAINS
RUINES
DRACULA
???
POULETS
AMÉRIQUE LATINE
NOUVEAUX PAUVRES
LAC DE LA TERRE DU MILIEU

L'ASIE VUE PAR LES USA

L'AFRIQUE VUE PAR LES USA

L'AMERIQUE DU SUD VUE PAR LES USA

LES CARAÏBES VUES PAR LES USA

L'OCÉANIE VUE PAR LES USA

DES OCÉAN
NOUILLES

LE TOMBEAU
D'OUSSAMA

GARDIENS DE
KANGOUROUS

LE SEIGNEUR
DES ANNEAUX

DENTS DE
LA MER

LE DIABLE
DE TASMANIE
(LOONEY TUNES)

LES ÉTATS-UNIS VUS PAR EUX-MÊMES

LÉGENDE

1. Catholiques
2. Nouvelle-Italie
3. Sardines en boîte
4. Savants fous
5. Statisticiens
6. Faux Français
7. Paradis fiscal

LES DICTATURES DU MONDE VUES PAR LES USA

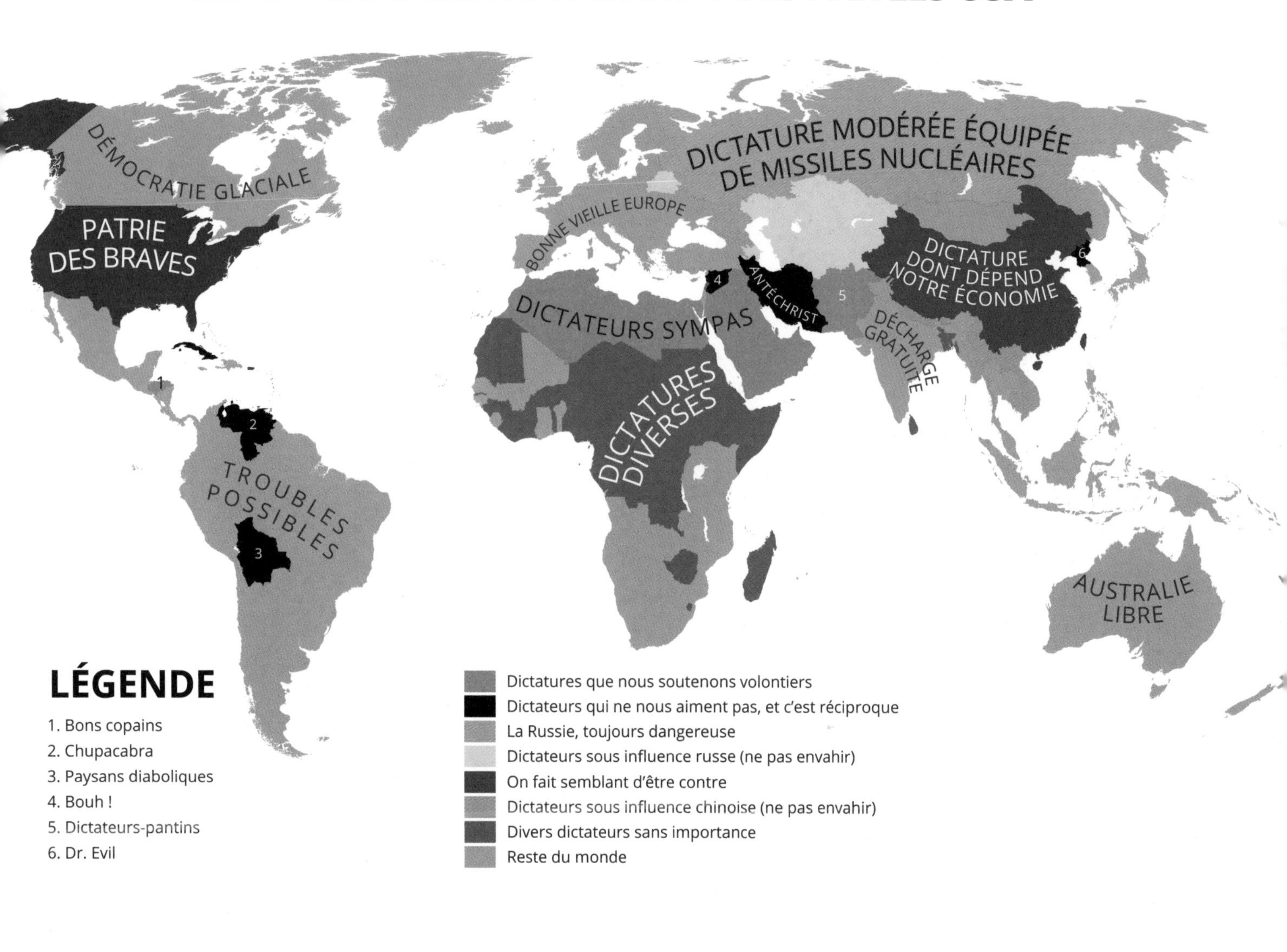

PÉTROLE

ROYAUME DU GRAND PAPE

INFIDÈLES

PÉTROLE

AVORTEMENTS

REPTILIEN

SATAN

HIPPIES

ÉVOLUTIONNISTES

PÉTROLE

ATHÉES

PELUCHES

ÉCOLOS

PÉTROLE

LA TERRE PLATE VUE PAR LES RÉPUBLICAINS AMÉRICAINS

LA TERRE DU MILIEU

Comme son étymologie l'indique, le propre d'une religion est d'unir les individus. Mais l'Histoire nous montre que l'homme voit des ennemis partout, même parmi ceux qui ont la même religion que lui.

Imaginez un peu : vous êtes un fan de Lady Gaga alors qu'apparemment le monde entier ignore tout d'elle. Et puis vous découvrez qu'elle a un autre admirateur. Vous n'êtes plus seul. Qu'allez-vous faire ensemble ? Trinquer à votre idole commune ou vous cracher à la figure avant de dégainer ?

Voilà ce que je n'arrive pas à comprendre quand on me parle du Moyen-Orient. Je sais qu'il y a de la politique là-dedans, et du pétrole, et plein d'épices, de chiche-kebabs, d'houmous et de citrons confits. Je lis les journaux.

Je sais aussi ce que pensent les chrétiens. D'après eux, la doctrine religieuse qu'ils ont, disons, adoptée, n'était pas exactement juive. Ils n'ont pas tort, parce que cette histoire de Jésus et Marie est une histoire égyptienne. Pour les musulmans, cette doctrine était d'abord juive puis on l'a déformée. Jusqu'à ce que le Prophète vienne remettre de l'ordre dans son interprétation. Croyez-moi, j'ai intérêt à croire à tout ça. Sinon... !

Même les juifs n'apprécieront pas si je leur rappelle qu'ils ont emprunté beaucoup trop d'idées au zoroastrisme.

Quant aux zoroastriens, je doute qu'il en reste beaucoup dans le monde, et que leur religion soit légitime : personne n'a été tué au nom d'Ahura Mazda depuis cinq cents ans.

Franchement, est-il possible de voir un lien entre ces histoires de croyances et de religions et une carte de géographie ? Elles se réfèrent à quelque chose de bien plus abstrait que le trottoir sur lequel vous vous déplacez. On y a peut-être cru autrefois, mais les civilisations qui les ont fait naître ont existé à des périodes très différentes de notre époque.

Pour elles, Jérusalem était le centre du monde. Aujourd'hui, seul un imbécile croirait que le centre d'une sphère est situé à sa surface.

Il semble que la Jérusalem terrestre soit en réalité aussi chaude que la surface du Soleil, qu'elle subisse une pression de 350 gigapascals et qu'elle soit située à 6 000 kilomètres sous vos pieds. Vous voulez trouver Dieu là-dedans ? Je vous souhaite bien du plaisir !

LE MONDE VU D'ISRAËL

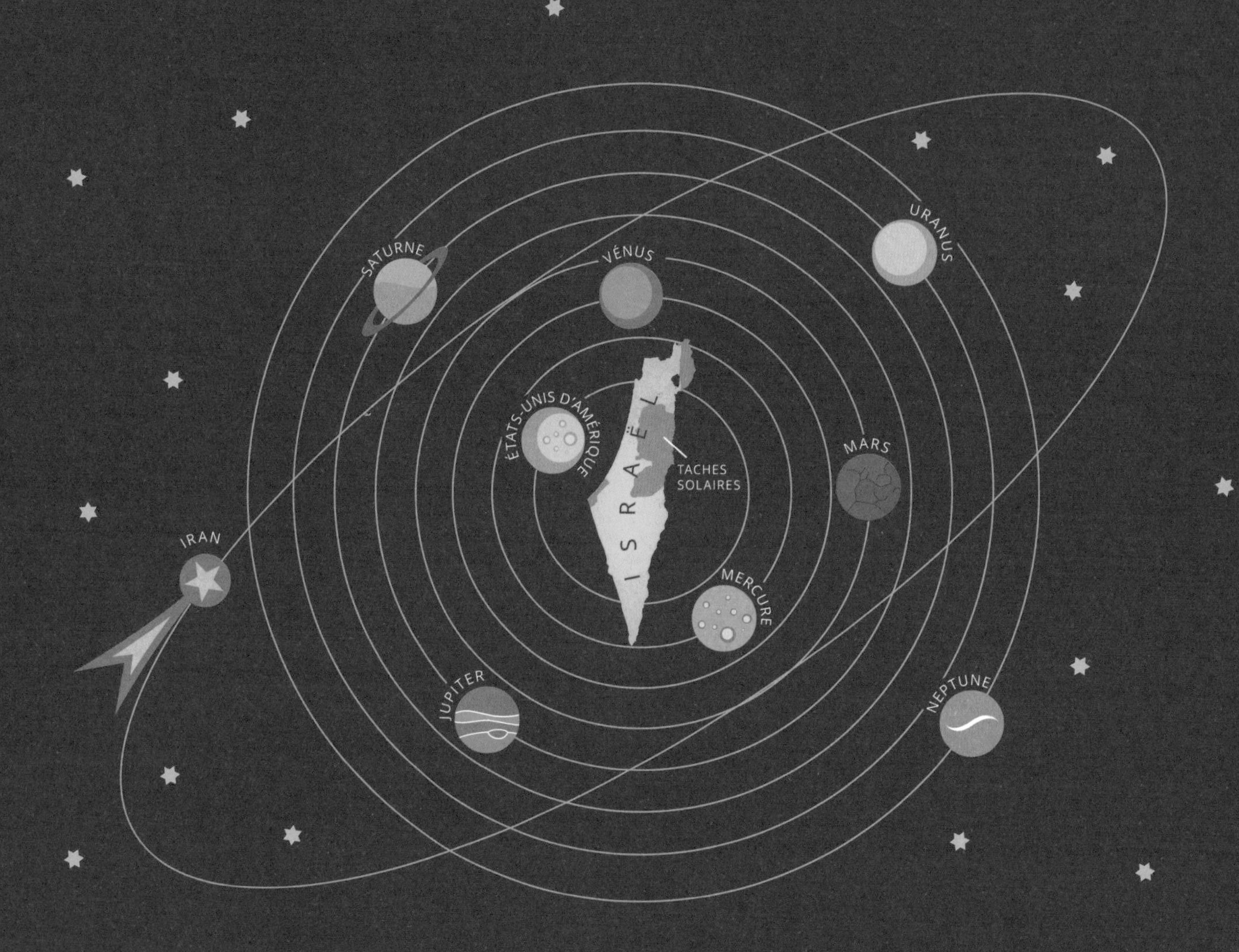

LE MONDE DE CHYPRE

LE PRINTEMPS ARABE 2011

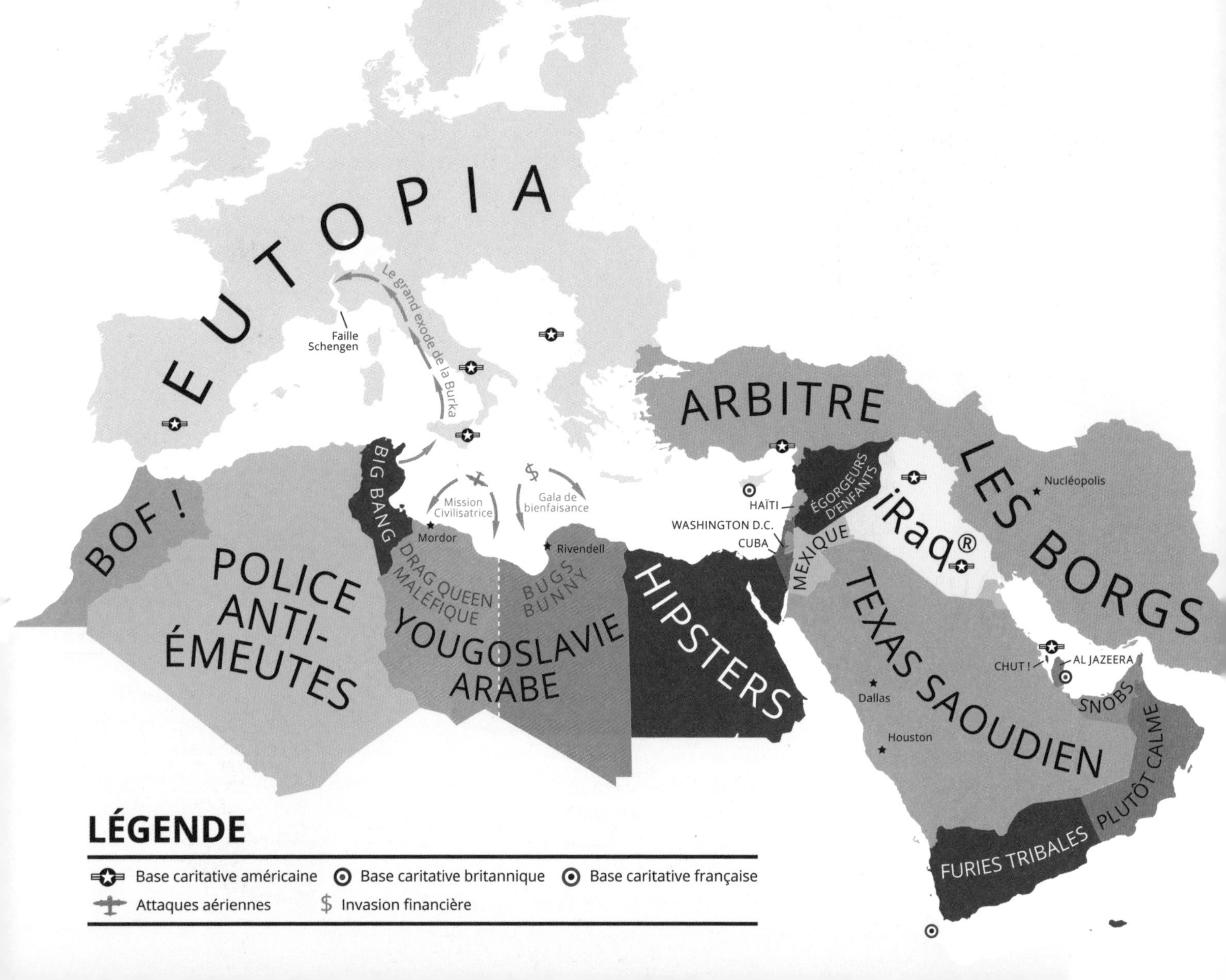

L'HIVER ARABE 2012

EUTOPIA
DÉMOCRATIE VOILÉE
PIÈGE À DRONES
Aire de stationnement
COUSCOUS ROYAL
DÉMOCRATIE ISLAMISTE
ACCROCS FIÉVREUX
PARANOS
CHEFS D'ÉTAT
MULES
MIETTES DE DÉMOCRATIE
PACIFISTES
GÉNÉRAUX MAFIEUX
DÉMOCRATIE TRIBALE
DÉMOCRATIE MILITAIRE
BANQUE CENTRALE DU TERRORISME
HUMM!
SNOBS
ENCORE CALME
TERRAIN D'ESSAI POUR DRONES US

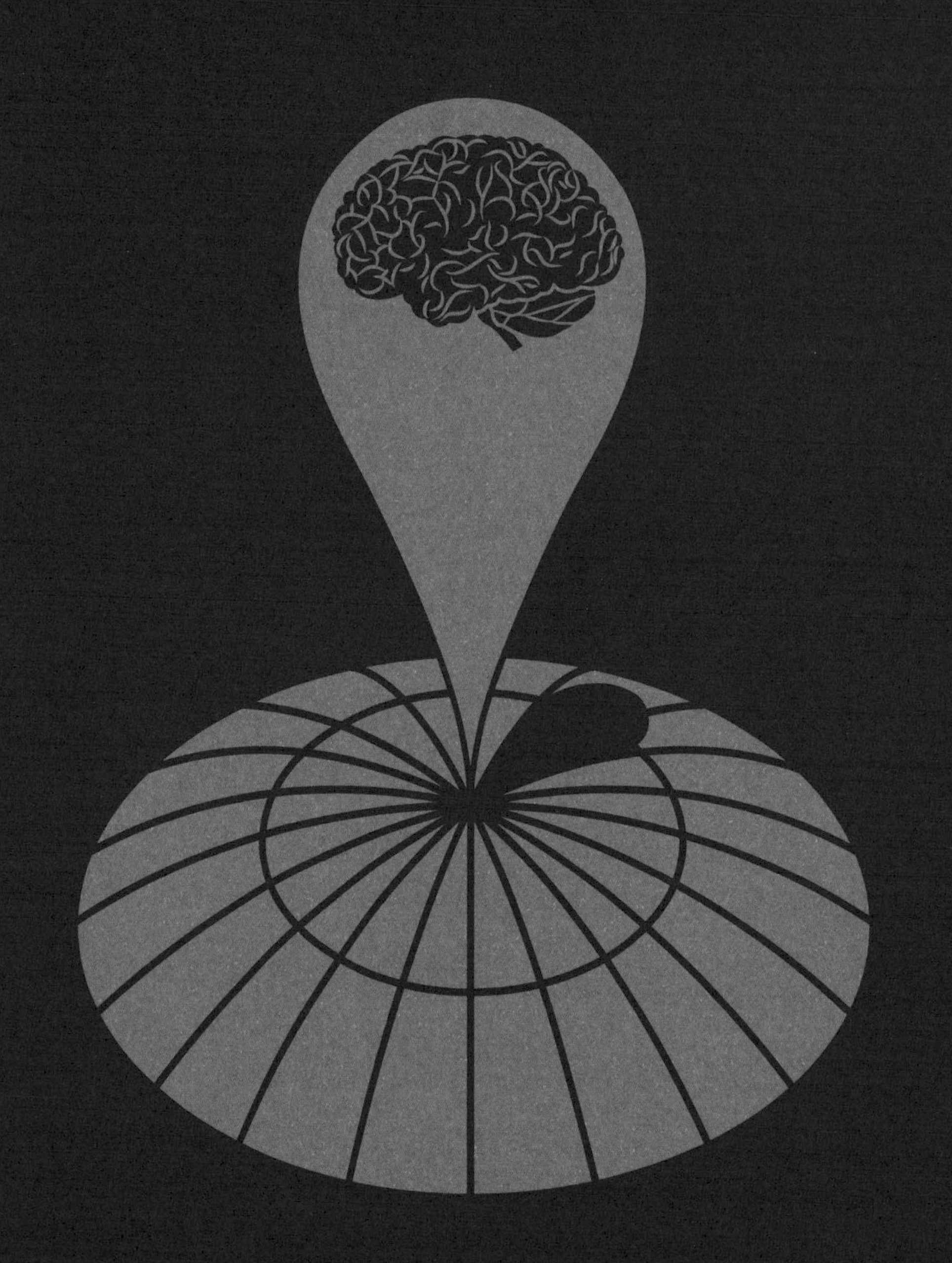

LA BOULE DE CRISTAL

Mon projet devant être présenté dans *The Guardian* au début de l'année 2012, j'ai eu un entretien avec un journaliste. Bien vite nous nous sommes mis à parler de la crise de la zone euro : avait-elle un impact sur le succès de mes cartes ? Je lui ai répondu que ce n'était pas leur intérêt qui avait changé, mais le contexte dans lequel les gens décidaient de les lire.

Avant 2010 on considérait ces cartes comme des gags. Peu à peu leur humour est devenu de plus en plus noir, jusqu'à ce que certains ne le perçoivent même plus du tout. Des Britanniques se sont mis à me féliciter pour avoir montré l'hypocrisie des fédéralistes européens, pendant que des Grecs me remerciaient d'avoir démasqué le néo-fascisme allemand… Je savais qu'un artiste redoute toujours de voir sa création déraper vers quelque chose de monstrueux, il fallait donc que j'évite ça à tout prix.

L'occasion s'est présentée quand le journal a suggéré que j'illustre l'interview avec de nouvelles cartes. J'avais fait une esquisse du futur de l'Europe mais je ne l'avais jamais terminée, faute d'inspiration. Elle dormait quelque part sur mon disque dur.

Mais, devant la montée du nationalisme en Europe, de nouvelles idées se sont imposées à moi et se sont multipliées comme des lapins. J'ai donc décidé de travailler sur le fantasme des ultra-nationalistes : l'explosion inévitable de l'Union européenne.

La carte est parue dans *The Guardian* en février 2012. Six mois plus tard, les journaux nationalistes catalans voyaient en elle la preuve que « la Catalogne est reconnue indépendante ». C'était assez embarrassant.

« J'ai tellement l'habitude de voir mon pays opprimé, ai-je lu sur Twitter, que même si c'est une blague, ça fait du bien ! »

Les opposants aux nationalistes s'en sont mêlés, accusant leurs compatriotes séparatistes de ne pas se conduire en patriotes. En réponse, j'ai laissé un message sur mon site disant que j'étais prêt à encourager toute solution pacifique et démocratique au problème.

Ça m'a servi de leçon : maintenant, j'y réfléchis toujours à deux fois avant d'oser ridiculiser les gens qui prennent les stéréotypes au premier degré. C'est le seul moyen de ne pas m'attirer d'ennuis.

L'EUROPE EN 2022

Bienvenue dans l'Europe du futur. Nous sommes en 2022, cinq ans après le Grand Schisme européen qui a mis fin au rêve de l'unité politique et économique du continent. Ça vous choque ? Je ne vois pas pourquoi. D'après une loi qui a fait ses preuves, l'Europe ne peut jamais rester unie trop longtemps. Elle explose toujours en son milieu, comme la bactérie qui se scinde afin de se multiplier. Les Empires romains d'Orient et d'Occident, les Églises catholique et orthodoxe, l'Est communiste et l'Ouest capitaliste : autant de scissions, autant d'échecs. Car l'unification politique et spirituelle du continent est impossible. Et 2022 finalise la dissolution de l'Europe d'aujourd'hui.

La zone euro va rétrécir jusqu'à devenir une entité, une fédération qu'on appellera Merkelreich. Elle comprendra l'Allemagne, la France, l'Autriche, et le Luxembourg. L'Italie, l'Espagne et la Belgique deviendront une mosaïque de petits pays, parmi lesquels le Pays Basque espagnol, la Wallonie belge, et l'Italie du Nord garderont l'euro et rejoindront le Merkelreich. L'Espagne va se désintégrer, la Galice et l'Estrémadure se tourneront vers le Portugal pour former avec lui la Portugalice. La Castille, région du centre de l'Espagne, deviendra le nouveau Vatican. Comme c'est là que vivent les catholiques les plus fervents, il serait logique que l'Église catholique change de territoire. Le reste de l'Espagne sera sous la coupe de l'Empire catalan, c'est-à-dire sous l'influence politique du Merkelreich.

L'Italie va rétrécir jusqu'à se réduire à la péninsule Apennine. La Sicile deviendra l'Alcatraz de l'Europe, où les criminels les plus dangereux seront déportés à vie. La Sardaigne sera une île à touristes, où les lois seront clémentes, et où les gens d'Europe Centrale et du Nord viendront se reposer chaque année. Les environs de Rome seront envahis par les gays, lassés de l'homophobie du Pape. Le Saint-Père sera assigné à résidence pendant un an, et on l'obligera à prendre des cours de samba. Et puis un jour il parviendra à s'échapper. Il s'enfuiera en Espagne, où le Nouveau Vatican sera proclamé lors d'une cérémonie grandiose à Valladolid. La partie occidentale de la Méditerranée deviendra la mer des Nudistes allemands, en l'honneur de tous les besogneux du Merkelreich qui continueront d'y aller chaque année. Compte tenu de la gestion exemplaire de leurs finances et de leur souci de l'épargne, aucun des citoyens du Merkelreich ne s'achètera un maillot de bain. Celui-ci étant considéré comme un accessoire anglo-saxon superflu porté seulement par des gens à la sexualité refoulée.

La Belgique éclatera, ou, plus exactement, n'arrivera pas à s'unir, et les Flamands iront rejoindre les Pays-Bas qui

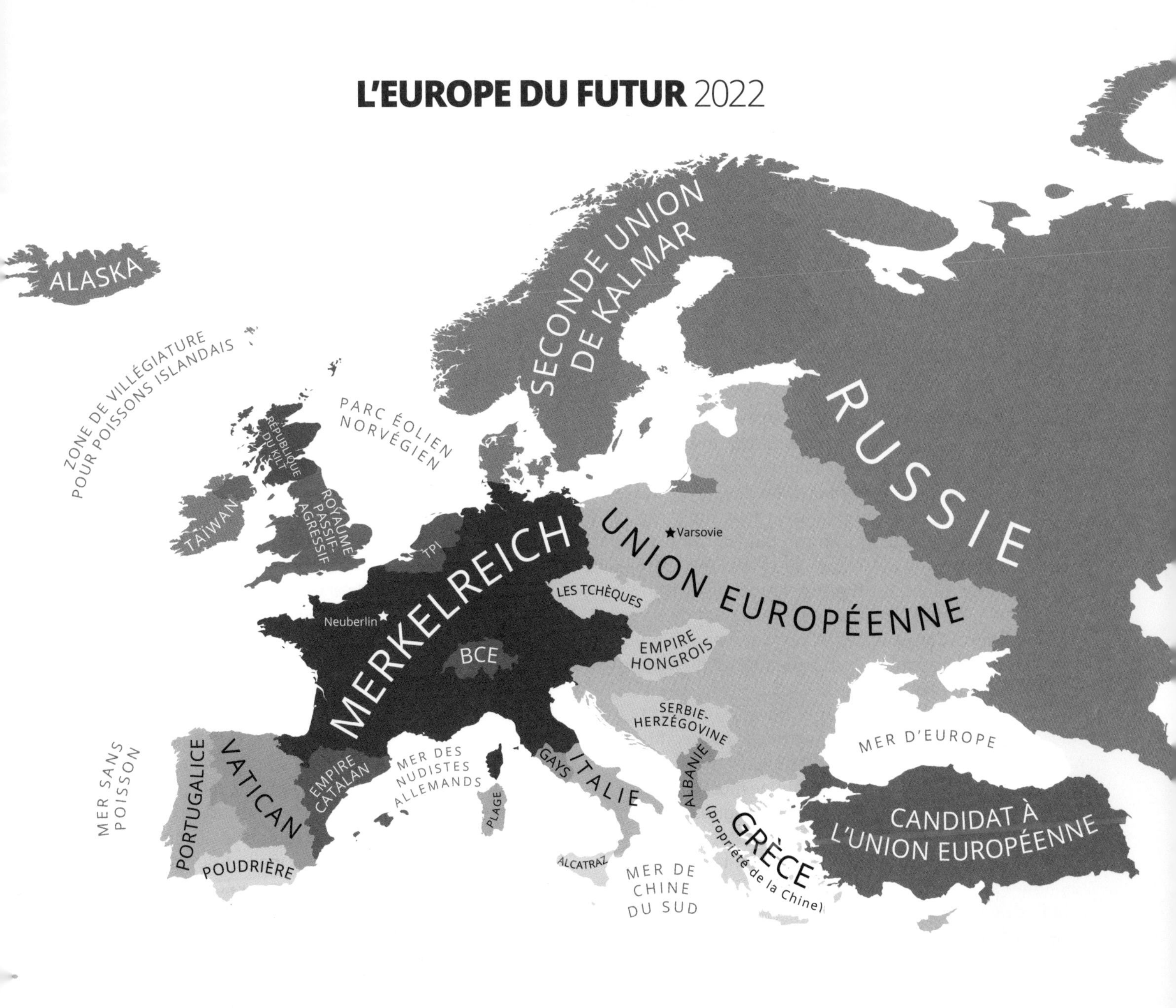
L'EUROPE DU FUTUR 2022
ALASKA
ZONE DE VILLÉGIATURE POUR POISSONS ISLANDAIS
PARC ÉOLIEN NORVÉGIEN
SECONDE UNION DE KALMAR
RUSSIE
RÉPUBLIQUE DU KILT
ROYAUME PASSIF-AGRESSIF
TAÏWAN
TPI
MERKELREICH
Neuberlin
BCE
UNION EUROPÉENNE
Varsovie
LES TCHÈQUES
EMPIRE HONGROIS
SERBIE-HERZÉGOVINE
ALBANIE
MER D'EUROPE
CANDIDAT À L'UNION EUROPÉENNE
GRÈCE
(propriété de la Chine)
ITALIE
GAYS
ALCATRAZ
MER DE CHINE DU SUD
PLAGE
MER DES NUDISTES ALLEMANDS
EMPIRE CATALAN
VATICAN
PORTUGALICE
POUDRIÈRE
MER SANS POISSON

laisseront tomber l'euro : les Hollandais n'apprécieront pas que leur pays devienne la côte Ouest du Merkelreich. Ils garderont la Cour internationale de Justice, ce qui maintiendra leur pouvoir judiciaire.

Leur pays deviendra une nation d'avocats qui seront sollicités partout sur le continent. Leurs prestations correspondront à la moitié des exportations hollandaises et seront responsables d'une grosse partie du PIB.

Les dirigeants de la zone euro se rendront compte qu'il n'y connaissent rien en affaires. La Banque centrale européenne sera transférée en Suisse qui, grâce à ses experts financiers, sera intégrée au Merkelreich, tout en gardant son indépendance sur le papier.

La nouvelle capitale du Merkelreich sera Paris, qu'on rebaptisera Neuberlin lors d'une cérémonie dans la galerie des Glaces à Versailles.

Au Nord, les pays scandinaves mélangeront leurs familles royales lors d'un mariage typiquement scandinave avec époux à volonté. Ils ne formeront plus qu'un seul pays, appelé la Deuxième Union de Kalmar*, qui aura trois rois, trois reines et une seule chambre royale. La Finlande et l'Islande deviendront respectivement des dominions de la Suède et du Danemark. N'étant pas des monarchies, ces pays ne seront pas représentés dans la famille régnante scandinave.

Les restes de l'Union européenne d'aujourd'hui inclueront l'Estonie, la Lettonie, la Lituanie, la Pologne, la Slovaquie, la Slovénie, la Croatie, Chypre, la Roumanie, la Bulgarie et la Macédoine. Cette dernière sera admise uniquement parce que la Grèce sera exclue. Cette Union européenne s'étendra vers l'Est pour inclure la Biélorussie, l'Ukraine et la Moldavie. Ainsi que la Voïvodine, qui sortira de la Serbie. La capitale de l'UE sera Varsovie, en hommage posthume au pacte de Varsovie et au Comecon communiste.

Il y aura trois États tampons en Europe centrale, coincés entre le Merkelreich et l'Union européenne. Les Tchèques, qui n'en font qu'à leur tête, quitteront l'UE. La Hongrie, trop autoritaire, en sera chassée. Elle deviendra un empire, et la fille de Viktor Orbán, son nouvel empereur, épousera le prince Harry. La Bosnie-Herzégovine et le Monténégro se joindront pour former la Serbie-Herzégovine, État chaotique où on pourra s'attendre à tout.

L'Albanie annexera le Kosovo et ensemble ils continueront d'être les pays les plus pauvres d'Europe. Au Sud, la Turquie maintiendra sa candidature à l'Union européenne, mais elle ne fera même plus semblant de vouloir y entrer. La Grèce fera faillite, financièrement et moralement, et je suppose que la Chine la colonisera bien vite. Les Grecs feront des statues de pacotille à la chaîne : elles iront décorer des villas en Chine et en Asie du Sud-Ouest. La partie orientale de la Méditerranée sera baptisée mer de Chine du Sud. Quant à la Grèce et aux États de l'Afrique du Nord, soit ils seront absorbés par la Chine soit ils deviendront des colonies.

Le même tourbillon gagnera les îles Britanniques : le Royaume-Uni se scindera en deux car l'Écosse votera son indépendence pour devenir une république. Tout ça pour embêter David Cameron. Plus tard, quand David Cameron sera devenu fou, les Écossais rejoindront la Couronne tout en restant indépendants.

L'Irlande aura du mal à choisir entre le Merkelreich et le Royaume-Uni. Cela aboutira à une impasse et le statut du pays restera indéfini. L'Irlande fera partie de la zone euro sur le papier mais pas dans les faits. Angela Merkel poursuivra une politique à la « deux systèmes pour un pays » mais le Royaume-Uni s'y opposera.

Voilà à peu près à quoi ressemblera l'Europe dans dix ans. Le continent sera dominé par deux super-puissances, le Merkelreich et la Russie, qui pèseront de tout leur poids sur l'Union européenne. Le Royaume-Uni restera isolé, au moins jusqu'au mariage de son prince avec la fille de l'empereur de Hongrie.

Le reste, comme on dit, appartient à l'Histoire.

**Union de Kalmar : qui a réuni en 1397 les royaumes de Norvège, Danemark et Suède.*

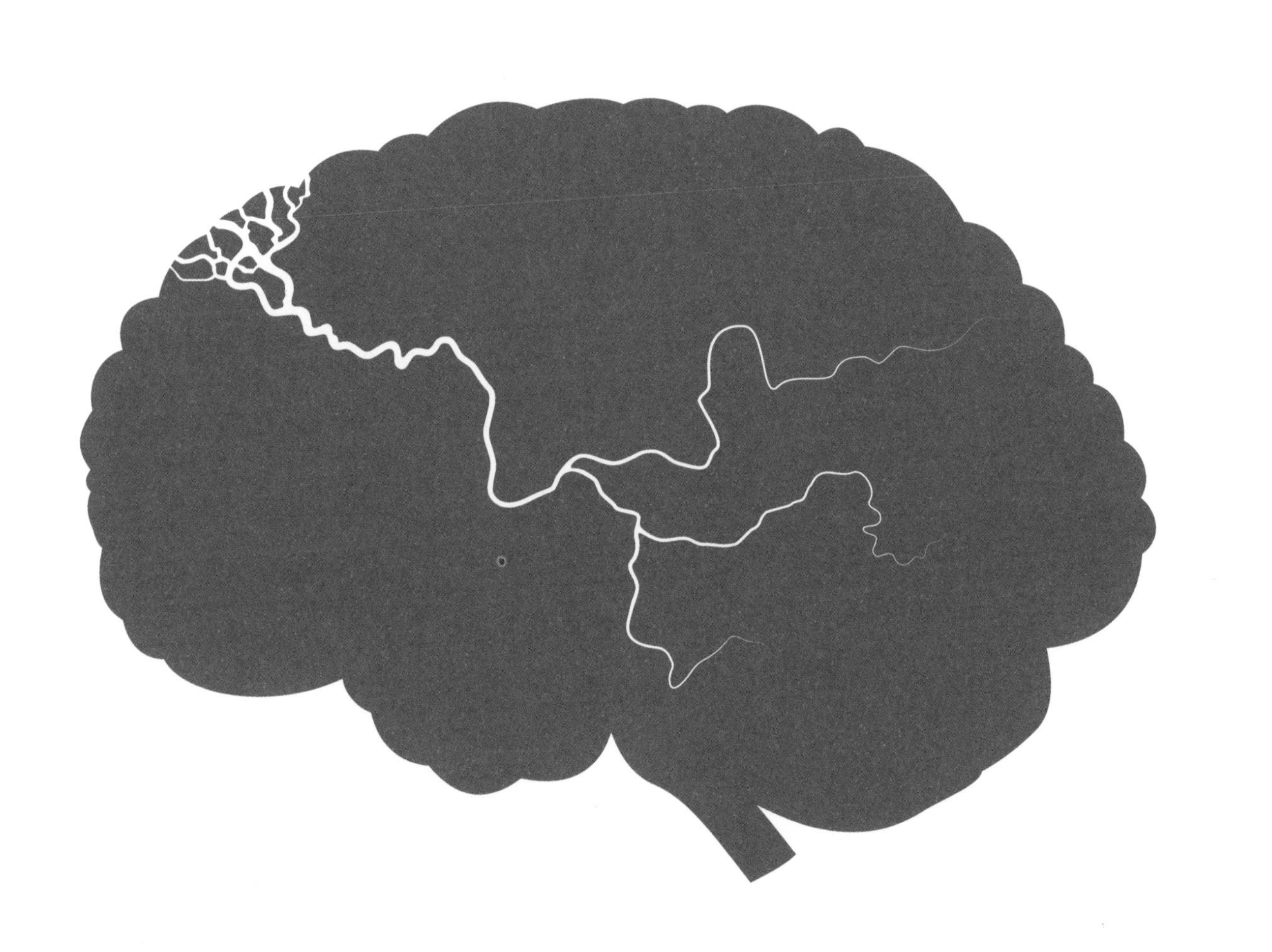

L'AUTEUR

Quand on lui demande de se présenter, Yanko Tsvetkov décline sa profession : explorateur, et son atout : la curiosité. Cette dernière est une richesse dont il a fait son métier.

D'origine bulgare, il est né en 1976 à Varna, au bord de la mer Noire. Élevé sous le régime communiste, il a grandi dans la crainte de Ronald Reagan et de son idée fixe, la guerre nucléaire.

Le début de sa puberté a été célébré de façon explosive : la catastrophe de Tchernobyl a eu lieu le jour de ses dix ans. Trois ans plus tard, quand les vents du changement ont balayé le communisme, on l'a envoyé dans une école où on enseignait la langue de Goethe. Il y a découvert beaucoup de mots utiles, parmi lesquels *lebensmüde* (« dégoûté de la vie »).

Il a ensuite rejoint la marine bulgare, où il a appris à diriger un bateau qui coule à l'aide d'un radar qui ne fonctionne pas.

Une expérience en cachant une autre, il a été tenté par le cinéma : son diplôme tout neuf de cinéaste a nourri son rêve fou de recevoir un Oscar un jour. Mais la lenteur de la production cinématographique ainsi que l'absence de spontanéité dans le 7e art l'ont vite déçu. Il a alors remplacé sa caméra par un ordinateur, tout en se découvrant une passion pour la photo, l'illustration, le design graphique et l'écriture. Il s'est baptisé *alphadesigner* et a créé son propre site.

Personnage cosmopolite, Yanko Tsvetkov a beaucoup baroudé, il s'est perdu dans des jungles touffues, il a transpiré dans des déserts brûlants et traversé en taxi des métropoles grouillantes. Ceci tout en apprenant quatre langues et en prenant des notes, soit sur papier, soit dans sa tête.

Mapping Stereotypes, son projet le plus connu, est né accidentellement en 2009. Un an plus tard, Yanko Tsvetkov était célèbre dans le monde entier. Depuis, il se régale de la dévotion de ses admirateurs, et reçoit parfois des courriels hostiles.

Sa devise est *« Never complain »* (« Ne te plains jamais »). Apparemment, il l'oublie très souvent.

NOTES ET REMERCIEMENTS

Ce projet est arrivé comme une grossesse imprévue. Et pour tout arranger je ne savais pas qui était le père.

Le bébé est sorti de moi tel un alien parasite. Comme il a modifié l'équilibre chimique de mon cerveau, je me suis attaché à lui, j'ai même pris soin de lui pendant son adolescence. Avant que je m'en aperçoive, j'avais concocté un livre que j'ai terminé à temps pour sa nuit de gala.

Je ne dirais pas que tout a été facile. Chez les gens qui ont des enfants, ceux-ci deviennent vite une excuse pour tout ce que leurs parents n'ont pas pu réussir. Le monde est plein de pères et de mères qui auraient pu réaliser de grandes choses, si seulement ils n'avaient pas été obligés de se lever tôt pour préparer le petit-déjeuner de leurs sales gosses.

Mon projet, je le détestais.

« C'est de ta faute ! À cause de toi je ne pourrai jamais faire une autre Mona Lisa ! », lui répétais-je.

C'est vrai, ça ! Trouvez-moi un seul artiste qui se soit révélé grâce à une carte ! Léonard de Vinci, d'après vous ? Il a gribouillé les choses les plus folles : des hélicoptères qui ne pouvaient pas voler, des planches d'anatomie dans lesquelles les artères reliaient les seins au vagin… Il a même peint *La Cène* sur un mur qui était tellement humide que les grenouilles pouvaient pondre leurs œufs dans ses fissures.

Et moi, qu'est-ce que j'ai fait ? Des cartes. Des interviews sur des cartes. Un livre sur des cartes. L'année prochaine, on me proposera peut-être de faire un film. Sur des cartes.

Heureusement pour moi, je suis entouré de gens qui m'empêchent de me plaindre tout le temps. L'un d'eux est Emiliano Barragàn, mon complice dans ce méfait, qui a refusé d'écouter mes jérémiades quand mon manque d'inspiration m'empêchait de commencer ce livre.

« Tu ne sais pas comment commencer ? Parfait ! Tu devrais écrire là-dessus ! » C'est un des meilleurs conseils que j'aie entendus !

Ce livre n'existerait pas sans l'enthousiasme et la patience de Martin Brinkmann, mon agent littéraire, qui pendant tout un été a supporté mes colères de diva. Quelle abnégation, pour un Allemand ! Sa foi en ce projet est sans limites.

Et surtout, je voudrais remercier toute l'équipe de chez Knesebeck, ma maison d'édition en Allemagne. Leurs encouragements m'ont donné confiance et, je crois, m'ont aidé à rester humble.

Achevé d'imprimé en Espagne
par Gráficas Estella à Villatuerta-Navarra en septembre 2014.